workers for the
harvest field

9:38
GOSPEL WORKERS FOR THE 21ST CENTURY

Edited by
Vaughan Roberts
& Tim Thornborough

THE
GoodBook
COMPANY

Workers for the harvest field
© The Good Book Company/ 9:38 2006

Published by
The Good Book Company Ltd
Elm House, 37 Elm Road
New Malden, Surrey KT3 3HB
Tel: 0845 225 0880; Fax: 0845 225 0990
email: admin@thegoodbook.co.uk
website: www.thegoodbook.co.uk

ISBN: 1 905564 30 9
ISBN 13: 9781905564309

Printed in the UK by Bookmarque

Contents

Introduction
Vaughan Roberts

> Jesus went through all the towns and villages, teaching in their synagogues, preaching the good news of the kingdom and healing every disease and sickness. When he saw the crowds, he had compassion on them, because they were harassed and helpless, like sheep without a shepherd. Then he said to his disciples: 'The harvest is plentiful but the workers are few. Ask the Lord of the harvest, therefore, to send out workers into his harvest field.'
>
> **Matthew 9 v 35-38**

PEOPLE TODAY ARE NO DIFFERENT to those Jesus met in the first century; they are 'harassed and helpless'. Can we see them as they really are, in all their desperate need? We are surrounded by those who are lost, separated from God and facing eternity without Him, 'like sheep without a shepherd'. Do we have compassion on them?

Jesus did. And His compassion led to action. He saw a vast harvest waiting to be gathered in, but hardly any workers to do the job. So He issued an instruction to His followers: 'Ask the Lord of the harvest, therefore, to send out workers into his harvest field' (Matthew 9 v 38).

That command still applies today. Although 2000 years of Christian witness have passed, there are still millions in our world who have never even heard the name of Christ. Vast areas of Asia, North Africa and the Middle East have been largely untouched by the gospel. Even in countries where many profess to be Christians there is great ignorance. There is still a desperate need for workers to be sent into the harvest field to reach the world and build the church. Ultimately, it is God who must send them (as Jesus does at the beginning of Matthew 10, sending out the twelve) but we are called to play our part as well. Jesus tells us to pray. That, in essence, is the 9:38 challenge. If we begin to see the world as Jesus sees it, we cannot do nothing. We must share our Lord's compassion and seek to do all we can for those who do not know Him. Will we commit ourselves to urgent prayer that He would be raising up, training and sending out suitably godly and gifted workers to serve Him in His world? And will we pray about our own role in this vital task?

This book is written for disciples of Jesus Christ who are willing to do just that. You have put your trust in Him and have received His gift of salvation. You know that all Christians are ministers of Christ, called to serve Him in the world and the church, and you have already begun to do that in various ways. But now you are wondering how you can best serve Him with the rest of your life.

These pages attempt to describe the nature of gospel ministry, and to answer the questions that those who are considering it may have. The aim is not to persuade everyone that they should give up their present jobs and offer themselves as workers to churches and missionary organisations. We all have different gifts. Some are suited to this kind of work, others are best used in other ways. We must resist the idea that some jobs are better or more 'spiritual' than others. But we should all be asking ourselves this question: 'What is it that I could do, as the person I am and with the gifts that God has given me, that would most bring glory to God through the spread of the gospel?' For some that will mean staying where they are; for others it will mean a significant change of direction. Before reading any further, spend a moment praying that this book would help you discern how best you can use your life for God's glory. And pray the prayer of Matthew 9 v 38: that God would send out workers into His harvest field.

SECTION 1:
What is gospel ministry?

What is gospel ministry?

Vaughan Roberts

A CHURCH LISTED THE NAMES of its staff members with their positions on its notice board. At the top of the list was the line: *Ministers: the whole congregation.* They had understood the Bible's teaching. The biblical word translated 'minister' simply means 'servant'. All Christians are called to full-time Christian service, serving Christ with the whole of their lives. This ministry, however, can take many different forms. In this chapter we will consider four pairs of characteristics to help us understand the nature of gospel ministry, which is one particular type of Christian service.

Gospel ministry

1. Two forms: universal and particular
2. Two priorities: word and prayer
3. Two roles: servant and leader
4. Two expectations: joy and suffering

---

1. Two forms: universal and particular

Gospel ministry comes in two forms. It is a responsibility for all Christian believers, but only some are set apart specifically for the task.

Universal: All Christians are called to engage in gospel ministry

As we will see, gospel ministry is the ministry of God's Word to both Christians and non-Christians. That is a task for us all. The responsibility of speaking to crowds of non-Christians is rightly entrusted to those who are especially gifted as evangelistic preachers or apologists. But all believers have the responsibility to make the most of the opportunities God gives us to share the gospel with our families, colleagues, neighbours and friends. Paul assumes that the whole Philippian church is to 'hold out the word of life' to the 'crooked and depraved generation' among whom they live (Philippians 2 v 15-16). And Peter tells his readers that they should 'always be prepared to give an answer to everyone who asks you to give a reason for the hope that you have' (1 Peter 3 v 15).

All Christians also have a ministry of God's Word in the church. It is not just the leaders or staff of a church who are to be engaged in pastoral ministry. We all have a responsibility to spur each other on in the Christian life with reminders of God's truth:

> Let us consider how we may spur one another on towards love and good deeds. (Hebrews 10 v 24)
>
> Encourage one another and build each other up. (1 Thess 5 v 11)
>
> Let the word of Christ dwell in you richly as you teach and admonish one another. (Colossians 3 v 16)

Particular: Some Christians are set apart for gospel ministry

When Titus was left by Paul on Crete to care for the young church that had just been established there, his first task was to appoint 'elders' in every town (Titus 1 v 5). They were not to be 'one-man bands', but rather, to function in teams. Elsewhere, these leaders are referred to as 'overseers', or 'bishops' (Acts 20 v 28; Philippians 1 v 1; Titus 1 v 7) and 'pastors' (1 Peter 5 v 2). The different titles are used interchangeably and speak of the same office. Some of the elders continued with other jobs, like Paul with his tent-making. Others were supported by the church to enable them to give all their time to the task (1 Timothy 5 v 17-18). Some churches today also employ children's, youth and women's workers and evangelists.

There is nothing that these workers do that is barred to other Christians. Their ministry is simply a particular expression of a universal responsibility. They are never called 'priests' in the New Testament. Since Christ, the great high priest, perfectly bridged the gap between us and His Father through His death on the cross, there is no longer any need for mediators between us and God as there was under the old covenant. The church does not have a priesthood; *it is a priesthood*. We are a 'royal priesthood' (1 Peter 2 v 9), called to be God's witnesses in the world. So there is no fundamental distinction between 'ordinary' Christians and those who are set apart for some form of gospel ministry. As we have seen, all Christians have a ministry, including a ministry of God's Word; but some are especially set apart for such a ministry.

2. Two priorities: word and prayer

Just before Jesus ascended into heaven He left some final instructions to His followers: 'you will be my witnesses in Jerusalem, and in all Judea and Samaria, and to the ends of the earth' (Acts 1 v 8). It must have seemed an impossible task for his tiny band of unimpressive followers, who just days before had deserted him after his arrest. But the command came with a promise: 'you will receive power when the Holy Spirit comes on you' (Acts 1 v 8). That power was evident in the dramatic early days of the church as it grew rapidly in Jerusalem and the surrounding areas. Even the threat of persecution made no difference. But then, in Acts 6, Luke records a potential crisis that threatened to arrest the advance of the gospel. A dispute arose over the church's distribution of food to poor widows, with the Grecian Jews complaining that their widows were being neglected, while the Hebraic Jews were well provided for. Everyone looked to the apostles to sort out the problem, but they refused to get involved.

As will become evident in chapter 3, there is no suggestion that caring for the poor in the church is not a Christian duty. The apostles knew that the job had to be done, but they were equally clear that they were not the ones to do it: 'It would not be right for us to neglect the ministry of the word of God in order to wait on tables' (Acts 6 v 2). The church was to appoint seven others to take responsibility for the widows so that the apostles could give their attention to 'prayer and the ministry of the word' (Acts 6 v 4). As a result, the crisis was averted. The church's leaders were not deflected from the two great responsibilities with which they had been entrusted. Consequently, Luke can write: 'so the word of God spread' (Acts 6 v 7).

A ministry of the Word

Gospel ministry is Word ministry. It is by His Word that God calls people to belong to Christ in the first place. Paul reminds the Ephesians: 'you also were included in Christ when you heard the word of truth, the gospel of your salvation' (Ephesians 1 v 13). It is also by His Word that we grow in our knowledge and love of Christ. Speaking of God's Word, Peter writes: 'Like new born babies, crave pure spiritual milk, so that by it you may grow up in your salvation' (1 Peter 2 v 2). If the world is to be reached and the church is to be built up, it is vital that many with gifts of teaching and preaching are set apart to minister God's Word and that they stick to that task and do not get deflected.

In his farewell speech to the Ephesian elders Paul exhorted them: 'Keep watch over yourselves and all the flock of which the Holy Spirit has made you overseers. Be shepherds of the church of God, which he bought with his own blood' (Acts 20 v 28). If we have been given oversight of other Christians, whether as a pastor, women's or youth worker or small group leader, we have the great privilege of caring for some of God's flock. The New Testament is clear that our chief responsibility is to provide them with good food by teaching God's truth from the Scriptures. Paul was a model for the Ephesian elders to follow. He reminded them: 'I have not hesitated to preach anything that would be helpful to you but have taught you publicly and from house to house' (Acts 20 v 20).

He urged Timothy, one of the leaders of the church in Ephesus: 'devote yourself to the public reading of Scripture, to preaching and to teaching (1 Timothy 4 v 13)... Preach the Word; be prepared in season and out of season; correct, rebuke and encourage—with great patience and careful instruction' (4 v 1-2). He also told Titus what kind of man he should appoint as an elder on Crete: 'He must hold firmly to the trustworthy message as it has been taught, so that he can encourage others by sound doctrine and refute those who oppose it' (Titus 1 v 9).

There is an urgent need for many more gospel workers who have a clear sense of the priority of God's Word. Others, both Christian or non-Christian, may provide food for the hungry, education for the ignorant and healthcare for the sick, but who will provide for their spiritual needs by pointing them to Christ? 'And how can they believe in the one of whom they have not heard? And how can they hear without someone speaking to them?' (Romans 10 v 14). Perhaps the church could do with a better magazine, tidier garden or bigger building; these are all valuable things to work at. But it *cannot* do without God's Word. So those entrusted with the task of teaching that Word must stick to it, even if that means disappointing congregation members who expect them to do a multitude of other jobs.

It may be that the youth group at the church down the road is bursting with young people, but that in itself is not a reason to copy its methods. Games, music and social events do not *in themselves* produce Christian disciples; that is God's work by His Spirit through His Word. And so, even if we organise a range of activities, Bible teaching must be right at the centre. We must maintain the priority of God's Word in all we do.

Prayer

The Lord Jesus was God incarnate and yet He still saw the need to pray. The gospels frequently refer to Him doing so (eg: Mark 1 v 35). The apostle Paul was also a man of prayer. He was a dedicated intercessor for the Christians in his care. For example, he told the Ephesian Christians: 'ever since I heard about your faith in the Lord Jesus and your love for all the saints, I have not stopped giving thanks for you, remembering you in my prayers' (Ephesians 1 v 15-16).

An Evangelical Alliance survey of pastors found that seven out of ten felt overworked. In a typical sixty-hour week they spent an average of twenty-two hours on administration, but only thirty-eight minutes in personal prayer[1]. Here is another fundamental aspect of gospel ministry that is too quickly pushed down the list of priorities. Alongside the ministry of God's Word, there must be a commitment to pray.

---

1 Quoted in Steven Croft, 'Ministry in Three Dimensions' p.17-18, Barton, Longman and Todd, London, 1999.

We should start by praying for ourselves. First and foremost I am a Christian, not a Christian worker. Unless I give time to nurturing my own relationship with Christ I will not be in a position to help anyone else grow in theirs. A book on secular leadership stresses the importance of 'sharpening the saw'. It tells a story of a man watching another try to cut down a tree with a blunt saw. He asks him: 'Why don't you sharpen the saw?' The reply comes: 'I haven't got time for that; I have to cut down this tree'[2]. The application in this context is obvious. If we are to have any hope of being sharp and effective in Christ's service we must spend conscious time in His presence, studying the scriptures and praying. As Thomas Chalmers wrote: 'no solid, permanent work of God can be expected where the piety and spirituality of the instrument is low, whatever His gifts may be.'[3]

As well as praying for ourselves and our own spiritual growth, we should also pray for those with whom we work. Once again, Paul is an inspiring and challenging example, not just by the quantity of his prayers but by their depth. He tells the Philippians: 'And this is my prayer: that your love may abound more and more in knowledge and depth of insight, so that you may be able to discern what is best and may be pure and blameless until the day of Christ, filled with the fruit of righteousness that comes through Jesus Christ—to the glory and praise of God' (Philippians 1 v 9-11).

Don Carson comments: 'Do you desire with all your heart what is best for the congregation you serve? Then you must ask yourself how much time you devote to praying this sort of prayer... Once our priorities are straight, we will learn to relegate tasks to their

---

2 Quoted in Croft p.112-113
3 Quoted in 'D Martyn Lloyd-Jones—the fight of faith' Volume 2 p.762, Banner of Truth, Edinburgh, 1990.

appropriate rank according to the values of scripture. Delegate some things; cancel others. You do not need to have a bulletin; you have to pray. You do not have to chair every committee or attend every meeting; you have to pray'.[4]

3. Two roles: servant and leader

Servant

All Christian ministry should flow out of the ministry of Christ to us. Although He was 'in very nature God' He 'made himself nothing, taking the very nature of a servant... and became obedient to death—even death on a cross' (Philippians 2 v 6-8). He 'did not come to be served but to serve, and to give his life as a ransom for many' (Mark 10 v 45). That example of sacrificial service is to be our model as we seek to follow Him.

As a young Christian, I was made President of the university Christian Union and began to think I was rather special. I was used to spiritual leadership so I imagined that I would be given an important job when I was asked to lead at a camp for teenagers that summer. In fact, my chief responsibility was to ensure that the toilet rolls around the site were frequently replenished. It was an important lesson. Whatever our position we are, above all, servants. Jesus said: 'whoever wants to become great among you must be your servant, and whoever wants to be first must be slave of all' (Mark 10 v 43-44).

Paul had a position of great authority as an apostle of Christ, but his preferred self-description was 'servant [or 'slave'] of Jesus Christ' (eg: Romans 1 v 1). He said: 'we do not preach ourselves, but Jesus Christ as Lord, and ourselves as your servants for Jesus' sake' (2 Corinthians 4 v 5). He served Christ by serving others. He

---

4 Don Carson 'Call to Spiritual Reformation' p.133, IVP, Leicester, 1992.

saw his work as a continuation of Christ's work, speaking of 'what Christ has accomplished through me' (Romans 15 v 18). He had no desire to gain a following for himself. His only goal was to glorify Christ by pointing others to Him.

At the height of his popularity as a guru, Bhagwan Shree Rajneesh had 93 Rolls Royces. When he was finally arrested by U.S. Marshals he was wearing 35 platinum and gold watches.[5] There are many like him, sadly even in Christian churches, who seek personal gain from religious leadership through prosperity, popularity or power. But we should be focused, not on what we can gain, but on what we can give. George Whitefield was probably the greatest of all British evangelists. He was a household name in the eighteenth century and yet he used to say: 'Let the name of Whitefield perish, so long as Christ is exalted'.[6]

Do we only imagine serving Christ in a comfortable area with which we are familiar or in a well-known church where we might make a name for ourselves? Or would we be prepared to go to another culture or a tough estate, where we could work for years, largely unnoticed? In our dreams for the future do we aim, above all, to serve ourselves or to serve Christ?

Leader

Most gospel workers have some kind of leadership role. That is certainly true of pastors. Paul urges the Thessalonians to 'respect those who work hard among you, who are over you in the Lord' (1 Thess 5 v 12). The writer to the Hebrews says: 'Remember your leaders, who spoke the word of God to you' (Hebrews 13 v 7).

---

5 Sunday Times 9th June 1996

6 J. C. Ryle '18th Century Christian Leaders' p.58, Banner of Truth, Edinburgh, 1978.

There is no contradiction between these two roles of servant and leader. If God gives us spiritual responsibility for others we should not allow a false humility to prevent us from fulfilling it. Christian leaders should lead. But they do so as servants, recognising that they are accountable to a higher authority. We may be 'shepherds of God's flock' (1 Peter 5 v 2), but Jesus alone is 'the Chief Shepherd' (1 Peter 5 v 4). We may have authority over others, but we should use it for their good, not ours: 'not greedy for money, but eager to serve; not lording it over those entrusted to you, but being examples to the flock' (5 v 2-3).

4. Two expectations: joy and suffering

I had two surprises when I started full-time gospel work. It was even better than I had expected; and yet it was also far harder. The words of John Newton and William Cowper in one of their Olney Hymns continue to describe my experience:

> *What contradictions meet*
> *In ministers employ;*
> *It is a bitter sweet,*
> *A sorrow full of joy.*[7]

Joy

After Paul had heard encouraging news from Timothy about the growth of the young Christians he had led to Christ in Thessalonica, he wrote: 'now we really live, since you are standing firm in the Lord. How can we thank God enough for you in return for all the joy we have in the presence of our God because of you?' (1 Thess 3 v 8-9).

---

7 Quoted in Handley Moule 'To my younger Brethren' p.1, Hodder & Stoughton, London, 1892.

The pastor who first encouraged me to consider gospel ministry told me: 'It's a never-ending job which is all-consuming and often exhausting, but it's an enormous privilege. I sometimes have to pinch myself when I think that I'm actually being paid to be doing something I love and would want to be doing anyway. It's a great thrill to spend most of my time engaged in a work where the fruit lasts for eternity'.

I could say the same. It is wonderful to see Christians growing to maturity in Christ, and nothing beats the excitement of being involved in another's conversion. One young man slipped a note under my door a day after we had had a conversation in which I had urged him to turn to Christ. It simply said: 'I've done it—it's wonderful!' There was joy in heaven, and there was great joy on earth too.

Suffering

Gospel ministry is certainly not all joy: there will also be suffering. Paul wrote to the Corinthians: 'death is at work in us, but life is at work in you' (2 Corinthians 4 v 12). Just as Jesus had to suffer and die before we could receive His gift of life, so His servants will endure much hardship as they seek to share His life with others.

If we set our hearts on doing some form of gospel ministry in the future, we desire a 'noble task' (1 Timothy 3 v 1). But not everyone will see it that way. The world will not be impressed by those who preach the weak and foolish message of Christ crucified (1 Corinthians 1 v 22-25). Like Paul, we can also expect opposition from within the church. He wrote: 'Up to this moment we have become the scum of the earth, the refuse of the world' (1 Corinthians 4 v 13).

We must not adopt an unrealistic, glamourised view of gospel ministry. Do not imagine yourself preaching to hundreds at a convention, or leading scores to Christ in a mission. It is not often like that. Most gospel ministry is a long hard slog. It is slow work with little visible fruit and, as Jesus teaches in the Parable of the Sower, even some of that does not last.

But we have good reason to persevere, even in the hardest times. Christ is with us by His Spirit, as He promised (Matthew 28 v 20; Acts 1 v 8) and one day He will return to gather in the harvest. Only then will we see the awesome results of gospel ministry down the ages: 'a great multitude that no one could count, from every nation, tribe, people and language, standing before the throne and in front of the Lamb' (Revelation 7 v 9).

The character required for gospel ministry

David Jackman

Here is a trustworthy saying: If anyone sets his heart on being an overseer, he desires a noble task. **1 Timothy 3 v 1**

PAUL IS ABOUT TO LAUNCH in to two chapters of teaching about the qualities required in the lives of those who are appointed to responsibilities in the servant-leadership of God's church. But before he reminds Timothy of the high level of demand, he first underlines that such a ministry is literally 'a good work' and therefore an appropriate object of aspiration.

However, for many Christians that sort of language sounds just a bit presumptuous. It smacks too much of putting yourself forward, which is not a greatly admired characteristic, even in our culture, let alone in our churches. Even though the apostle Peter says that those who shepherd God's flock as overseers, should serve 'not because you must, but because you are willing, as God wants you to be' (1 Peter 5 v 2), we are still hesitant. We can think of all sorts of reasons not to pursue personally the possibility of full or part-time paid Christian ministry, and many of them may well be valid.

Individuals may certainly become convinced that this is not the right direction for their lives, but the process of discovery in itself is important to work through. No-one comes out of a serious assessment of their gifts, skills, temperament and ambition without being made more aware of their strengths and weaknesses, more confident of God's providential direction of their lives, and more dependent on His limitless grace to serve Him wherever, whenever and in whatever He chooses. The question, then, is not whether it is right to seek the 'noble task' of the overseer, but rather, whether we are willing to begin the adventure with God of seeking to discover how we can serve Him best. Many young Christian men are still only too ready to pray: 'Lord, here am I; send my sister' (with apologies to Isaiah 6 v 8). Assuming that you are ready for the challenge, let's see what the Bible has to say about the tasks and the qualifications needed.

Bible roots

It is often said, and quite legitimately, that every Christian is 'in the ministry', since we all want to serve our Lord Jesus Christ, and all that we do in our lives can and should be offered to Him as our 'spiritual worship' (Romans 12 v 1). One of the strongest biblical justifications for this view comes from the metaphor of the church (all who have repented and put their faith in Christ, as rescuer and ruler) as *the body of Christ*. This is especially developed by Paul in key New Testament teaching passages like 1 Corinthians 12 v 12-31 and Ephesians 4 v 1-16.

The foundational truth here is that **all Christian ministry is Christ's ministry, exercised through His people, in the power of the Holy Spirit.** The church on earth can, therefore, be compared to the limbs of a body, exercising a multiplicity of different functions, but all under the direction and control of the head. So, Paul can tell the Corinthians, in common with all Christians everywhere: 'Now you are the body of Christ, and each one of you is a part of it' (1 Corinthians 12 v 27). The great commission given originally to the eleven disciples in Matthew 28 v 16-20 has not been rescinded, since its command and promises are declared to be valid 'to the very end of the age', which we have not yet reached.

Not surprisingly, the twin responsibilities to make Christ known, through declaring the gospel and living godly lives which confirm the message, keep recurring throughout the New Testament letters. The Philippians are exhorted to 'shine like stars in the universe as you hold out the word of life' (Philippians 2 v 15-16). The Thessalonians are singled out for special commendation because 'the Lord's message rang out from you... your faith in God has become known everywhere', so 'you became a model to all the believers' (1 Thessalonians 1 v 7-8). Peter exhorts his readers to 'always be prepared to give an answer to everyone who asks you to give the reason for the hope that you have' (1 Peter 3 v 15). There are multiple instances of such teaching and exhortation, which indicate that every believer has the responsibility for 'gospel ministry', in the sense of seizing whatever opportunities present to testify to who Jesus is, and to confirm the reality of the truth by a life of love and godliness. Thus far, every Christian is included in Christ's call to follow and serve. So why should some be set apart to be paid to do what every Christian has a responsibility for?

Suitable candidates

It is not clear exactly how or when the setting apart of individuals for ministry, with their support coming from the gifts of others, first began. Its origins probably lie in Jesus' call to the disciples to leave their daily work and follow Him (e.g. Mark 1 v 16-18, 2 v 14), and certainly by Luke 8 v 3 we find a group of women who were 'helping to support (Jesus and His disciples) out of their own means'. Paul is quite clear that 'the Lord has commanded that those who preach the gospel should receive their living from the gospel' (1 Corinthians 9 v 14). Indeed, he states categorically that this is the accepted practice with 'the other apostles and the Lord's brothers and Cephas' (1 Corinthians 9 v 5), although he has deliberately chosen to forego this right for himself, so that 'in preaching the gospel I may offer it free of charge, and so not make use of my rights in preaching it' (1 Corinthians 9 v 18). Clearly, the practice of paid ministry goes back to apostolic times and there are indications that this may have applied not only to the travelling apostles and their delegates, like Timothy or Titus, but also to local congregational elders, as when Peter exhorts them to be faithful under-shepherds, 'not greedy for money, but eager to serve' (1 Peter 5 v 2).

But on what grounds were such appointments made? Who were the suitable candidates? Here, the pastoral epistles to Timothy and Titus give us some valuable insights. For example, Titus was commanded by Paul to stay in Crete, after its initial evangelisation, to 'appoint elders in every town' (Titus 1 v 5). There then follows a list of qualifications by which Titus is to assess potential candidates. The striking feature is that they are detailed qualities of character, in three full verses (v 6-8), followed by only one verse (v 9) on theological reliability.

Twice, Paul stresses that the overseer, whom he describes as 'entrusted with God's work' is to be 'blameless', which cannot of course mean perfect, but someone who cannot be reproved, whose character is transparent and whose integrity is well-known. Positively, he is to be 'one who loves what is good, who is self-controlled, upright, holy and disciplined' (v 8b). Negatively, his life is to be manifestly 'not overbearing, not quick-tempered, not given to drunkenness (that is lack of self control), not violent or pursuing dishonest gain' (v 7). And the place where you will see what kind of man he really is will be in his home, with his wife and children (v 6). When these qualities are in evidence, then holding firmly to the truth 'so that he can encourage others by sound doctrine and refute those who oppose it' (v 9) becomes the final, and of course essential, qualification for appointment. But isn't it significant that character comes first?

Exactly the same priorities can be observed in the longer parallel passage in 1 Timothy 3, dealing with both elders and deacons. Beginning again with the requirement that the overseer is to be 'above reproach', from verses 2 to 7 Paul explores what that means, almost exclusively in terms of personal character. There is only one gift mentioned, 'able to teach', which is essential; but the emphasis is on a man's character. 'He must also have a good reputation with outsiders' (v 7a). The only other concern is that 'he must not be a recent convert' (v 6a), since pride in being elevated to such a responsibility too soon may prove to be his downfall, as it was the devil's. Similarly with deacons, 'they must first be tested' (v 10), and here again, character (v 8) precedes doctrinal orthodoxy (v 9), though, for Paul, the two are inextricably linked. 'They must keep hold of the deep truths of the faith with a clear conscience' (v 9).

Such leaders are seen to be the gifts of the ascended Christ to His church, as foundation gifts in the shape of the apostles and prophets for the earliest believers, but continuing in the roles of evangelists and pastor-teachers through all the generations of the church's existence in this world. This is Paul's teaching in Ephesians 4 v 7-11 (see also 2 v 20 and 3 v 5), recognising that God's governing purpose is 'to prepare God's people for works of service (ministry), so that the body of Christ may be built up... attaining to the whole measure of the fulness of Christ' (4 v 12-13). So, we are most likely today to see these functions fulfilled in the work of the evangelist/church planter and the pastor/teacher, for whom the provision of financial support, to enable them to devote their full time to these tasks, is entirely appropriate. In this way, the body of Christ will mature, growing and building itself up in love (Ephesians 4 v 13-16), so that 'now, through the church, the manifold wisdom of God should be made known to the rulers and authorities in the heavenly realms' (Ephesians 3 v 10). The New Testament minister devotes his life to reaching the lost with the gospel and building up the saved, so that the church becomes the living prototype in time-space history now of what God will accomplish with His renewed creation throughout eternity, 'to bring all things in heaven and on earth together under one head, even Christ' (Ephesians 1 v 10).

Clarified agenda

Ministry is, then, no easy task. It is very far from being a job which any reasonably keen Christian might like to try, as an escape from spending one's working days in our hostile and godless culture. And yet, it is undoubtedly true that not a few young Christians are drawn towards 'ministry' for precisely those reasons. The danger will always be that we are attracted towards ministry with the wrong motives, for how it will benefit us and what we may get out of it, and we need to be ruthlessly honest with ourselves about the strength of such temptations.

When Paul commissioned the Ephesian elders, at his final meeting with them, recorded in Acts 20 v 17-19, his keynote instruction was: 'Keep watch over yourselves and all the flock of which the Holy Spirit has made you overseers. Be shepherds of the church of God, which he bought with his own blood' (v 28). This metaphor of shepherding as the key to understanding the nature of biblical ministry runs all the way through the Scriptures. God Himself is the great Shepherd of His people Israel in the Old Testament (think of Psalm 23), and yet He always used human channels to accomplish the task. So, Psalm 77 ends with the verse: 'You led your people like a flock by the hand of Moses and Aaron' (v 20). Then, the next psalm, Psalm 78, concludes: 'He chose David his servant and took him from the sheep pens...and David shepherded them with integrity of heart' (v 70-72). At the very least, this means that David's example is of a shepherd who risks everything to protect and nurture his flock, whose service is not for his own benefit, but for the well-being of the sheep.

Ezekiel 34 reveals that this is precisely what the 'shepherds of Israel' (the leaders both politically and religiously) did not do, and it was a major contributory cause of the exile to Babylon. 'Woe to the shepherds of Israel who only take care of themselves!', the Lord says. 'Should not shepherds take care of the flock?' (Ezekiel 34 v 2). Instead of strengthening the weak, tending the sick and searching for the strays, they stand accused by the Lord of harsh and brutal rule, eating the curds, clothing themselves with the wool and even killing the best animals (v 3-5).

As a result, God's flock is 'scattered over the whole earth' (v 6). But eventually, God sent great David's greater Son, the Good Shepherd who laid down His life for the sheep (John 10 v 11) and so fulfilled the promises made through Ezekiel, centuries before. 'I myself will search for my sheep and look after them... I myself will tend my sheep' (Ezekiel 34 v 11-16). 'My servant David will be king over them, and they will all have one shepherd' (Ezekiel 37 v 24). The Lord Jesus, who is the good shepherd, knows His sheep by name and they follow Him (John 10 v 14, 27), so He is also described in the New Testament as the Chief Shepherd (1 Peter 5 v 4) and 'that great Shepherd of the sheep' (Hebrews 13 v 20). He becomes the model shepherd, on whom all His under-shepherds must pattern their ministry, since all authentic ministry is Christ's, exercised through His people and in the power of His Spirit.

The danger will always be that the under-shepherds assume their role for the wrong motives, governed by their own desires and ambitions, and the flock is then used as the proving-ground of their ministry. The signs of this will be the absence of the characteristics of the good shepherd—love, true humility and service, a willingness to sacrifice for the good of others—which are the hallmarks of Christ's ministry. These are the qualities of character for which God is searching, if ever real gospel ministry is to be exercised in the church. When Jesus came to Israel during His incarnation He did not find such shepherds. As in Ezekiel's day, the flock was still scattered and oppressed. 'When (Jesus) saw the crowds, he had compassion on them, because they were harassed and helpless, like sheep without a shepherd' (Matthew 9 v 36). In many sections of the church today, the situation seems much the same. That is why 9:38 is so called. It picks up the response of the Lord Jesus in the next two verses of Matthew 9, recognising that a plentiful harvest needs many more workers to gather it in. 'Ask the Lord of the harvest, therefore, to send out workers into his harvest field' (v 38). The metaphor changes, but the priorities remain the same.

9:38 began its life to help bridge the gap between the first stirrings of desire to be a harvester, or an under-shepherd, and the eventual deployment of the equipped and trained labourer in the harvest field, or as the under-shepherd of the flock. This process often begins in early adult life, at university, or during a first job. God sets our hearts on fire with love for Christ and the gospel, and we long to spend all our time in doing the work which invests for eternity. This is often a period of wonderful enthusiasm and vitality, when a 'go anywhere, do anything' outlook prevails. The last thing I, or any responsible Christian leader, would want to do is to pour cold water on that fire. But there does have to be a period of 'proving', before the expensive investment of training for a lifetime in paid ministry is undertaken. A 'recent convert' (to use Paul's warning to Timothy in 1 Timothy 3 v 6) can be pushed too far too soon, which will open up all sorts of temptations to arrogance, reinforced by a desire to cover insecurity. The parable of the sower, or better, the soils, in

Luke 8 v 4-15, warns us soberly that not every promising beginning is matched by continuance. 'They believe for a while, but in the time of testing they fall away' (v 13). Student life provides some degree of testing, but it is likely to be much more challenging in the world of employment and that provides a necessary proving of both the faith and perseverance of the new convert.

Under-shepherds need to have been proved to be faithful, dependable sheep, and this is largely a matter of character. God is not usually in as great a hurry as we are, in our busy, task-focused world. Ripening is a process which takes time and which includes rain as well as sunshine. And God is looking for maturity, ripened godliness, rather than spectacular gifts and abilities, in His 'work force'.

Personal priorities

Have you noticed how the New Testament ministry emphasis is so often not on *what* is done, but *how* it is done? Just as our personal godliness is the greatest contribution any of us can make to the evangelisation of our generation, so the ministry which most accurately reflects the character of Christ will bring the greatest glory to His name. Truly obedient service is always motivated by truly grateful love. So, it is an essential part of coming to a sober estimate of ourselves and our abilities (Romans 12 v 3), to be as honest as possible about why we want to do what we want to do.

I remember an interview with an applicant for the Cornhill Training Course, where an undoubtedly keen, young Christian was holding forth (at length!) about how he loved to study the Bible and loved to teach it to others. He was brought up rather short by my colleague's enquiry: 'And do you love the people you teach it to?' For that lies at the heart of all Christ-like service. 'A good minister of Christ Jesus,' Paul tells Timothy, will not only expose false teaching, being nourished in the truths of the faith, but will devote himself to its outworking in his own life: 'train yourself to be godly... Don't let anyone look down on you because you are young, but set an example for the believers in speech, in life, in love, in faith and in purity...Watch your life and doctrine closely' (1 Tim 4 v 6-16). This whole passage will repay careful study.

There is a real danger that the attraction of in-depth Bible study, to an able academic mind, may propel that person towards paid ministry, even though the other necessary gifts and character qualities may not be in evidence, or at least, not yet. I have sometimes heard the view expressed that if you have the brains to get a degree and a conviction about the truth of the gospel, then you need to provide very good reasons for *not* going into paid ministry.

But is that so? It is all too easy to jump on to a sort of conveyor-belt fresh from graduation, with a local-church apprenticeship, or participation in a training course, leading straight on to theological or Bible-college training, and emerging at the end 'ordained' to minister. What can be omitted, sadly, is the 'proving' time of living in an ordinary job, as an ordinary church member, deepening one's relationship with Christ in those contexts, rather than always as a trainee leader. 9:38 exists to support, encourage and challenge people through those years of 'proving', whenever they happen, by keeping ministry possibilities at the top of the agenda, through its conferences and other materials. It also aims to provide sounding-boards by which gifts can be tested, temperaments assessed and 'sober judgments' arrived at. This avoids the danger of playing up training for ministry in the areas of academic ability and success, at the expense of godly character and servant-heartedness. Of course, we want the best equipped work-force possible for the demanding challenges of ministry in the contemporary climate, but we must at the same time resist the seduction of academia, which imagines that more degrees automatically ensure better training for ministry. Wherever academic competition begins to dominate theological training, something is going badly wrong.

The reason for this is not hard to identify. It is that the godly practice of Christ-like ministry is profoundly counter-cultural. This is because it is the expression of a self-giving love, which is *others-centred*, rather than focusing on *me*, as the practitioner. It is not that we can or should expect the finished article here and now so that only those who are perfect need apply for ministry. Wasn't it Spurgeon who said that he had only known one 'perfect' man and he was a perfect nuisance? No—Paul told Timothy: 'Be diligent in these matters; give yourself wholly to them, so that everyone may see your progress' (1 Timothy 4 v 15). What needs to be assessed and proved is steady progress in godliness of character, as the indispensable qualification for ministry. Only that will keep us persevering for the long haul, which is so much needed today, when too many who are in ministry in their twenties are out in their thirties, or early forties.

Character checklist

It may help to end this chapter by looking through a brief, biblical, character check-list, and seeking honestly to evaluate one's motives and abilities in the light of them. Take time to do this prayerfully and involve a trusted friend and one of your church leaders to work with you and help you through the assessment. Remember, it is not a finished product we are looking for but what Eugene Petersen described the Christian life as: 'a long obedience in the same direction'.

1. **Am I prepared to be Christ's devoted disciple**, by denying myself and taking up the cross to follow Him, ready to surrender my life to Christ and the gospel? (Mark 8 v 34-35)

2. **Will I commit myself to Jesus,** as Lord and Teacher, by a life of humble service, as exemplified in His washing of His disciples' feet? No servant is greater than his master. 'I have set you an example that you should do as I have done for you' (John 13 v 12-17). 'Clothe yourselves with humility towards one another... Humble yourselves under God's mighty hand' (1 Peter 5 v 5-6).

3. **Do I honestly accept Paul's assessment** of all who plant and water the good seed of the gospel in God's field, that we are 'only servants, through whom you came to believe'? The Lord assigns the tasks and we all have the one purpose: 'So neither he who plants nor he who waters is anything, but only God, who makes things grow' (1 Corinthians 3 v 5-9). And will I recognise that this must spell the end of all confidence in the flesh? 'For who makes you different from anyone else? What do you have that you did not receive? And if you did receive it, why do you boast as though you did not?' (1 Corinthians 4 v 7).

4. **Can I embrace the values of Christ's 'upside-down' kingdom and by His grace make them my lifestyle?** 'The greatest among you should be like the youngest, and the one who rules like the one who serves... But I am among you as one who serves' (Luke 22 v 24-27).

These are the roots of a godly character, which will issue in the fruit of the Spirit (Galatians 5 v 22-23), seen in a life and ministry able to impact both the church and the world, as Christ reveals Himself through His servant. To set one's heart on this is, indeed, to desire 'a noble task'.

The priority of gospel ministry

Richard Coekin

[1] In those days when the number of disciples was increasing, the Grecian Jews among them complained against the Hebraic Jews because their widows were being overlooked in the daily distribution of food. [2] So the Twelve gathered all the disciples together and said, 'It would not be right for us to neglect the ministry of the word of God in order to wait on tables. [3] Brothers, choose seven men from among you who are known to be full of the Spirit and wisdom. We will turn this responsibility over to them [4] and will give our attention to prayer and the ministry of the word.'

[5] This proposal pleased the whole group. They chose Stephen, a man full of faith and of the Holy Spirit; also Philip, Procorus, Nicanor, Timon, Parmenas, and Nicolas from Antioch, a convert to Judaism. [6] They presented these men to the apostles, who prayed and laid their hands on them.

[7] So the word of God spread. The number of disciples in Jerusalem increased rapidly, and a large number of priests became obedient to the faith. **Acts 6 v 1-7**

My friend Justin is a talented young man with a promising medical career. He is also a very godly leader and able Bible teacher. He and his new wife are both mature Christians, currently free of family responsibilities, and they face a difficult decision. Their church pastor has asked Justin to consider changing direction to train in gospel ministry as a professional pastor-teacher. What should he do? What biblical principles should Justin, and others facing similar decisions, bear in mind?

Two kinds of ministry

It is helpful to remember that, essentially, all Christians have two kinds of 'ministry' (service) for the Lord. We all serve the Lord's purposes for this world as we contribute where we can to the biblical government of this planet. We do this as we play our part in the wise stewardship of the earth's resources, the just government of the world's nations and the improvement of the welfare of all humanity, especially the poor, weak and vulnerable. We might call this our 'creation ministry', serving God's purposes for this creation.

But all Christians also have a second kind of 'ministry' for the Lord. We serve the Lord's purposes for the world to come. We contribute what we can to the extension of the kingdom of God in the hearts of mankind through the gospel. Whenever we explain the gospel in conversation, Bible groups or pulpit, in the boardroom, hospital ward or classroom, we are engaged in this 'gospel ministry' that serves God's purposes for the new creation that is coming.

Both 'creation ministry' and 'gospel ministry' are serving the Lord. It is an important biblical principal rediscovered in the European Reformation, that there is no divide between the 'secular' and 'sacred'. The medieval church taught that we serve God better by leaving the 'secular' world to become a monk or nun in the 'sacred' world of the convent or priory. But the Bible teaches that we may worship God in all facets of life in sacrificial holiness. Our Lord Jesus, the perfect servant (or 'minister'), apparently did this with the hard manual labour of a tradesman or carpenter. And so Alistair McGrath can fairly conclude: 'We could summarise the Reformation attitude to work as follows. In serving our fellow human beings, we are glorifying God. Work is an act of praise. There is a God-given dignity to human work. To become a Christian does not entail withdrawing from the world, but committing oneself to that world with a new outlook.' [1]

However, this does not mean that all our ministries for the Lord are equally important. One can polish shoes, mow the lawn or darn socks 'for the Lord' (ie: with holy motivations) just as one can run a *Christianity Explored* course for unbelieving neighbours 'for the Lord'. But if we had to choose between them, for example choosing whether to spend a Thursday evening mowing the lawn or explaining the gospel to our neighbours, most Christians instinctively recognise that, while both are serving the Lord, one takes priority over the other. Our ministry of lawn mowing might improve our local reputation for having a tidy garden. But our gospel ministry might save someone from hell.

In this simplistic situation, the lawn will have to wait. Unfortunately, most decisions are not so black and white. It is not always obvious that a young doctor should become a pastor-teacher—there may be many factors that bear upon such a decision. But the Bible does make one principle clear. It plainly emphasises that our 'gospel ministry' of seeking to save people from hell for heaven is generally more important and takes priority over our 'creation ministry' seeking to improve people's lives in this world. This is clear in Scripture from the purposes of God, the ministry of Jesus, the commands of the apostles and the relative benefits of each.

---

1 Alistair Mcgrath, *Roots that Refresh*, Hodder & Stoughton, 1992.

- **The purposes of God:** We find that God's love is expressed, above all, in saving us: 'For God so loved the world that He gave His one and only Son, that whoever believes in Him shall not perish, but have eternal life.' (John 3 v 16). We enjoy God's love in His provision for life in this world, but chiefly, in redeeming us for the next. Gospel ministry is God's priority.

- **The ministry of Jesus:** Jesus described His own priority to be gospel ministry. 'For the Son of Man came to seek and to save what was lost.' (Luke 19 v 10); or 'For even the Son of Man did not come to be served, but to serve, and to give his life as a ransom for many.' (Mark 10 v 45). Jesus instructed all who are His disciples to do likewise: 'he must deny himself and take up his cross and follow me' (ie: suffering for the salvation of others, Mark 8 v 34); and: 'Therefore go and make disciples of all nations...' (Matthew 28 v 19). Gospel ministry was Jesus' priority.

- **The commands of the apostles:** Peter says: 'Always be prepared to give an answer to everyone who asks you to give the reason for the hope that you have' (1 Peter 3 v 15); Paul says: 'I am not seeking my own good but the good of many, so that they may be saved. Follow my example.' (1 Corinthians 10 v 33 – 11 v 1). Gospel ministry was the apostles' priority.

- **The relative benefits of each:** the eternal benefits of gospel ministry seem to clearly outweigh the more temporary benefits of creation ministry. Put crudely, while medical help can delay death for a few years, it is only gospel ministry that can rescue us from an eternity in the horrors of hell for an eternity of joy in the new creation. The priority of gospel ministry is clear from the relative benefits of each.

We see this theological principle worked out in practice in the famous early-church crisis described in Acts 6 v 1-7.

Acts is the second volume of Luke's carefully researched 'orderly account' of the saving ministry of Jesus Christ (Luke 1 v 1-4). In Acts, he records how Christ empowered His disciples with His Holy Spirit to be His witnesses 'in Jerusalem, and in all Judea and Samaria, and to the ends of the earth.' (Acts 1 v 8). Acts tells us how the gospel spread through the preaching of the apostles, especially Peter and then Paul. In the early chapters of Acts, we read how Christ enabled the early church to overcome three obstacles to the advancement of the Word of God: first, the external persecution of the church (chapters 3-4), then, the internal corruption of the church (chapter 5) and now, by the subtle distraction of the preachers of the church (chapter 6). We learn here how the apostles resolved a tension arising between their 'creation ministry' (critically important relief work) and their 'gospel ministry'. In so doing, Luke has recorded for us an example of how the apostles applied the priority of gospel ministry to their lives.

1. Their problem was distraction

The apostles had been administering a common fund for the poor of the church (4 v 35; 5 v 1). But as 'the number of disciples was increasing' (v 1) a distressing injustice emerged. The 'Grecian Jews' (Christians who were Jews with Greek language and culture) realised that the widows from their community, who now depended on the church, rather than the Temple relief food to survive, were being neglected by the 'Hebraic Jews' (Christian Jews from the Hebrew culture) in the daily food distribution. There was, unsurprisingly, 'complaining' about this.

This was a really serious problem for obvious reasons. There had been prejudice and suspicion between these communities in the past, and it would undermine the Christian claim that the gospel was for all peoples if this prejudice was seen to be continuing in the church. Moreover, this was a serious need. These widows, unable to work and buy food for themselves, were liable to starve without urgent help. And this would be of huge personal importance to the apostles. No doubt they knew many of these women personally— they'd been converted in recent months under their preaching. It was really tragic to hear of this problem (even if it had arisen out of poor administration or communication, rather than prejudice). This was a serious issue. Something had to be done. But not by them!

When the twelve apostles 'gathered all the disciples together', they revealed their great anxiety that meeting this relief need would inevitably distract them from their ministry of the Word and prayer. They perceived a serious problem in being distracted from the gospel ministry by which many were being saved and the church was growing, even by this urgent need for better social administration of relief work.

The truth is that all believers face this problem. Christians working in offices often find that the growing demands of their jobs can begin to distract them from their evangelistic relationships or homegroup preparation. Christians working at home may find themselves distracted from evangelistic opportunities by excessive domestic burdens. Pastors who should be preparing sermons get distracted by many worthy meetings discussing important strategy, pressing personal issues and administrative crises of varying kinds. And some who could be maximising their gospel ministries by working part-time to run a Mums & Toddlers group, or could go abroad with a mission agency to help plant churches, feel unable to do so because of distracting 'creation ministry'. Like many others, Justin felt he was being distracted from maximising his gospel ministry by the 'creation ministry' of his medical career. Some people can use their 'creation ministry' as an excuse for not maximising their 'gospel ministry.' Christian teachers, nurses, postmen and bankers who witness to Christ by 'life and lip' are so precious. We need more such workers. But above all, we need more Christians to be set free to devote more of their time to gospel ministry. As Jesus observed: 'The harvest is plentiful but the workers are few.'

Some young people who are free to change direction in ministry are deceived by the health of their own churches. They don't realise how few churches in this country can regularly enjoy saving Bible-teaching. They don't realise how many millions, even in this country, have never heard the gospel explained in language they understand. And neither do they realise that many areas of the world have little access to any gospel teaching at all

One of Thomas Hardy's most delightful *Wessex Tales* is *The Distracted Preacher*. It tells of a young preacher who went to stay in a seaside village inn in Cornwall for theological study. But he was distracted by the inn-keeper's daughter and soon fell in love with her. It's an enchanting tale but illustrates a very serious problem of the distraction of the teachers of the Word of God, which the apostles took steps to address. Too often today, potential gospel ministers are being distracted by their creation ministry from maximising their gospel ministry. Their problem was distraction.

2. Their priority was the ministry of the Word and prayer

The apostles gathered the church together to explain their theological priority: 'It would not be right for us to neglect the ministry of the Word of God in order to wait on tables'. If something is not right, it is wrong—the words 'to wait on tables' are literally, 'to serve' or 'to minister' to tables. This food distribution was a 'ministry' for God just as much as the 'ministry' of the Word. Both are ministries. And the apostles didn't suggest that the poor widows should be neglected—something must be done, urgently—*but not by them!*

So why mustn't they do it? They must have wanted to! Some have suggested that this was the unique responsibility of the apostles—that the apostles had to concentrate upon teaching the Word, but nobody else should do the same today! This cannot, however, be the explanation because they do not say it would be wrong to neglect 'the ministry of an apostle' but wrong to neglect 'the ministry of the Word of God', the 'gospel ministry', which all Christians have with varying opportunity to exercise it.

Alternatively, some have called this a matter of 'calling', as if the apostles were 'called' to this by God, while others are called to famine relief, so that we must also respect our own calling. The trouble with this language of 'calling' is that although we may be given by God a sense that we feel spiritually more comfortable about exercising a particular kind of ministry, the Bible uses this language of 'calling' differently. The call of God comes through the gospel to become a Christian, and not to a particular job or ministry. Our feelings are notoriously unreliable. And we can use the language of 'calling' to unnecessarily delay others, as well as ourselves, from maximising or prioritising gospel ministry.

So why did the apostles say it was wrong to neglect their ministry of the Word? They said it was wrong because they were applying the theological priority we have examined—the ministry of the Word of God takes priority over the other kinds of ministry we perform for God. We can worship God in all areas of life, but proclaiming the gospel is the most important of all. In the end, 'creation ministry' may delay death but only 'gospel ministry' saves from the punishment of hell. We find this same priority in Jesus' ministry (which is presumably where the apostles learned it).

In Luke 4, for example, after Jesus had healed many people (4 v 38-41), He went out to pray and then, when asked to stay, He replied: 'I must preach the good news of the kingdom of God to the other towns also, because that is why I was sent.' And He kept on preaching! When confronted with a paralysed man (Luke 5 v 17-19), He addressed the man's deepest need by forgiving his sins, because forgiveness is our greatest need. We know that Jesus could heal from afar. He could have spent years emptying the hospitals of Judea and addressing the fairer distribution of resources and the corruption of the Roman Empire. He certainly did heal those He came across in His preaching tours, to identify Himself as the promised Messiah and to demonstrate the renewed condition of His kingdom to come (Isaiah 35). But He was evidently reluctant to reverse the judgment on this world, groaning in its corruption and frustration, until He returns with the kingdom of God.

This certainly does not constrain the alleviation of suffering in this world, which Jesus demonstrated everywhere He travelled preaching. But it does establish that Christ's priority was clearly preaching the gospel, for by it, people are saved into the new creation, eternally free from sickness and death.

Indeed, preaching the gospel is the best welfare strategy for this world from two perspectives. First, the gospel brings the power of the Holy Spirit into people's lives, so that they repent from wicked behaviour that causes so much pain and distress others, and begin to live in righteousness and justice and love. Secondly, it gives access to an eternal world where there is no more death or mourning or crying or pain. So, although the relief brought by 'creation ministry' is wonderful, the relief brought by 'gospel ministry' is far more wonderful. That is why Jesus pursued 'gospel ministry' as a priority, instead of 'creation ministry'. This is not the world's priority; but it is Christ's. The world will never applaud missionaries the way it applauds famine relief workers. We do need more Christian famine-relief workers, but we need more gospel workers even more urgently. We all need to maximise our gospel ministry as the people God has made us, with the opportunities God has given us. The apostle Paul put this priority in military terms: 'No one serving as a soldier gets involved in civilian affairs—he wants to please his commanding officer (2 Timothy 2 v 4). I don't see why this dedication should be interpreted as applying only to clergy. All Christians have Word ministry to be maximised.

The world will never value evangelism above charity. Christ has shown that He values both. But when competing for our attention, our faith in the gospel of salvation from the judgement to come (Romans 2 v 16) puts gospel ministry first in our lives. So, from Jesus, the apostles realised that when 'creation ministry' and 'gospel ministry' are competing for our time and attention, the ministry of the Word of God must generally take priority. They would have to do the one and not do the other.

Of course most of us can often do both. We can take every opportunity we get to preach the gospel, and we can also pursue creation ministries of mercy like famine relief. But for some people and on some occasions, such as for my friend Justin, we have to choose which ministry to exercise and which to neglect, because we can't do everything. For example, when I was a commercial solicitor in London I used to help run a youth club for boys in Bethnal Green. For a while I managed to do both. But as my involvement at the youth club and opportunities to preach the gospel elsewhere began to multiply, I was starting to neglect my ministry at work in order to exercise my gospel ministry. I couldn't do both. Which should I choose? Jesus and His apostles taught that the ministry of the Word of God takes priority. For me to maximise gospel ministry, I had to give up my work as a solicitor so I could devote myself full-time to becoming a pastor-teacher. Not everyone can do this—but I could. And if I could, Jesus and the apostles' priority showed me that I should.

An interesting illustration of this priority is found in the life of the great American evangelist, D.L. Moody. During the Civil War, in the Battle of Shiloh (or Pittsburgh Landing) in 1862, Moody joined a boat coming down the Tennessee River. He found 450 badly wounded men, many soon to die. What would we try to do in such a ghastly scene? Moody and his companions made up their minds: 'We would not let a man die on the boat without telling him of Christ and the forgiveness of sins.' Rather than dedicate themselves solely to the tragic health needs confronting them, they resolved to address the deepest need of those suffering soldiers—for gospel ministry.

The tragic scenes of starving children in need of famine relief are familiar to us from television news reports. But we also need to watch God's television set with pictures of the nations of this world, wealthy and poor alike, starving for want of the bread of life who is Christ. It is not that we must become less concerned for those who need physical bread. We need to be more concerned for them. But we must also realise that the even more pressing need of the world is for the saving gospel of Christ. Usually we can help with both. But it is wrong to neglect the ministry of the Word of God that feeds people who are starving for lack of the bread of life, even for the sake of famine relief.

Their priority was the ministry of the Word and prayer.

3. Their proposal was delegation

But the apostles didn't leave their hungry church unfed. They ensured that the need would be met, but not by them.

They consulted with the church to find the finest and most reliable men to whom they could delegate this 'ministry of tables', men full of the Spirit and of wisdom, ie: godly and able men. So often, we find it hard to delegate important ministry to others. Pastors find it hard to trust others or to lose control. Sometimes church members can be lazy or expect the preachers to do everything. But this church understood the priority of gospel ministry and were pleased by the proposal (v 5). They chose men with Greek names (perhaps those better able to understand people from Grecian culture), who were of such quality that some, like Stephen (the first martyr), and Philip (the evangelist), emerged with wider gospel ministry as well. They were approved by the apostles, commended to God in prayer, and authorised publicly to their vital new ministries. It is important to notice that in applying the priority of Word ministry, the apostles didn't leave creation ministries of mercy neglected. They took the trouble to delegate carefully to others.

Here was a spiritually healthy church in which those with Word ministry were willing to delegate to others important but distracting alternative ministries. The church members were willing to accept and volunteer to relieve their hard-pressed pastors of those ministries, to ensure they were properly done.

The result of this solution is summarised in v 7: 'So the word of God spread'. It is clear that Luke intends us to understand that the Word spread because of the delegation of distractions. If the ministry of the Word is neglected, the Word of God will not spread. Where, conversely, pastors and others with gospel ministry can dedicate themselves to the ministry of the Word and to prayer, the Word of God will spread. This summary is the first of six such summaries (9 v 31, 12 v 24, 16 v 5, 19 v 20, 28 v 30) at critical points in Luke's account of the growth of the church and the spread of the gospel. This first critical point involves the dedication of those with opportunity for Word ministry to the work of the Word and prayer. (It is indeed striking that the terms used, 'spread' and 'increased rapidly', echo the command of God at creation, 'Be fruitful and multiply'. This is because the spread of the gospel spreads the rule of Christ, God's King, and so extends His kingdom rule, which is what humanity was originally created to ensure. 'Gospel ministry' actually accomplishes the essential 'creation ministry'!)

It is important to notice that the growth of the church and the spread of the Word followed the twin implications of the priority of gospel ministry: those with word ministry concentrated on their ministry and others were found to feed the poor of the church. The Word was properly preached and the widows were properly fed! The Word spread because the people of Jerusalem both heard clear sermons and witnessed practical love in the church. It was not just good talks and it was not just famine relief. It was both, initiated by those with opportunity for Word ministry, leaving distracting creation ministry to others.

Let me outline some simple conclusions for those considering gospel ministry like Justin:

1. We must all seek to maximise both our creation ministry and our gospel ministries (both are service to God) but where they compete for our time and resources, our gospel ministry takes priority over our creation ministry;

2. We must all grieve over community dysfunction and long to address the needs of the world with God's love. But the most precious gift we can give to our broken communities and pain-wracked planet is the gospel. Through the gospel, all may be adopted into God's loving family, transformed by His power and enjoy the hope of His new creation, free from pain and injustice;

3. If we have gifts and opportunity for developing our gospel ministry, we must be willing to delegate other good but distracting ministries to others, so that we will not neglect our ministry of the Word to serve 'at tables'.

My friend, Justin has, rightly, I believe, concluded that he must 'delegate' his workplace medical ministry to others in order to maximise his gospel ministry by training to become a pastor-teacher. God plainly doesn't want everyone to leave regular employment for gospel ministry employment, because most people will not have the gifts or opportunity to be able to be paid for gospel ministry. But those that could must be willing to delegate their creational work to others. Some will need to realise that, though they may have some openings for the gospel in their workplace, there are many more for those set apart for gospel ministry full time. Many gifted young people would pursue gospel ministry if they could. Churches must make it easy for more to do so.

If we have a choice, we must recognise the priority of Word ministry established in Scripture and practised by the early church. All Christians need to maximise their gospel ministry. For most of us, this will mean searching for every opportunity in our work, in our social engagements and in our friendships to talk about Jesus Christ. But for some of us, it may now mean considering a change of employment.

Each of us needs to recognise where we or others are being distracted from the ministry of the Word and prayer by other good ministry that should be delegated to others. When we apply the priority of gospel ministry, by the grace of God we too could observe:

'So the word of God spread. The number of disciples... increased rapidly.' **Acts 6 v 7**

SECTION 2:
Varieties of gospel ministry

The pastor-teacher

Andy Gemmill

> If anyone sets his heart on being an overseer, he desires a noble task. **Paul to Timothy**

> 'Are these people with problems?' **An unnamed medical practitioner**

'Are these people with problems?' I don't think I have ever been asked a more memorable question. I remember the situation (over a body in casualty), the questioner (a more senior medical colleague) and the occasion (he had just heard that my next job was not going to be treating patients in the NHS but leading Bible studies in a local church). I remember the facial expression—my colleague's that is—the tone of voice, and especially, in one usually measured and rather reserved, the unguarded speech. The question popped out with the raw vigour of projectile vomit. He just couldn't keep it in.

One can see why. What could be so worthwhile about leading Bible studies, which makes that a better thing to do than medicine? Is there something about those people which makes that a really noble thing to do?

I have often thought about his question. For me, it has come to encapsulate so many of the biggest issues involved in changing career from a professional job to the world of church ministry and, over the years, at good times and bad, his question has been added to by a host of my own, many of them rather less than noble.

- *Why exchange something obviously useful for something which isn't?*
- *Why exchange something I knew I could do, for something which so exposes my weaknesses?*
- *Why exchange a role with social status for one with little?*
- *Why exchange something easily measurable (kill or cure!) for something hard to measure?*
- *Why exchange financial reward for less?*
- *And what about these people? Are they people with problems... and what does that make you?*

In this chapter I want to say something about the work of being a pastor-teacher in a local church. In particular I aim to address those issues which are specially relevant for anyone considering the choice between this work and what one might call a 'regular' career. I have in mind two groups of people: those who are already thinking about what that work might involve, and whether they should be making that move; and those who aren't but ought to be.

My chief aim is to convince you that, as a friend put it to me, 'The responsibility is magnificent,' and that for the right person, there is nothing better, more exacting, more stimulating and ultimately more glorious than the work of bringing God's word to bear on the lives of a congregation of God's people.

Your situation

My guess is that if you're thinking of getting involved in church leadership, and have read even this far, certain things will probably be true of you. You will be a bloke in your 20s or early 30s (although there are increasingly opportunities for older men as well). You will have been serious about being a Christian for between 5 and 10 years. You have possibly been to university, and been involved in the work of a Christian Union. Since then, you have joined an evangelical church of some description, though you are unlikely to have been there for more than 5 years. At church you have been helping with some aspect of the work, maybe with children, teens or students. You will have done a bit of small-group Bible study work, may have led an evangelistic course, and have given the odd talk ('not too odd' was the feedback) to small groups of people.

What is almost certain is that your life will be getting measurably more complicated year on year. You may be married or thinking about it; you may have small children. Your finances are more stretched than they have been before. You may have taken out a mortgage. It is almost certain that demands in your work are growing significantly and that you are finding it more difficult to fit everything into life. So what of being a pastor-teacher?

Reasons for uncertainty

It is difficult for most people, given these circumstances, to imagine ever being a local church pastor. There are three main reasons for this. First, there is a significant gap between your current level of experience in ministry and that needed to do the job. For example, when you are only used to preaching an occasional sermon, the idea of preaching every week seems a long way out of reach. It is not always easy to see how such gaps can be bridged.

Second, there may be a growing gap between your relative competence in your regular job and your competence in ministry. In your job the learning curve is steep, you are receiving training and gaining experience, you are gradually growing in confidence and ability. It is unlikely that this growth is being matched in your church situation. So the longer you go on in your work, the more able and confident you become, and the scarier the prospect of changing direction seems.

Third, let's face it, there's the job itself! Who would want to be a church minister; to deal with all those people, all those problems; to be responsible for it all? Who would want to be public property like that? The reality is that for many of us the role of pastor-teacher may seem unattainable, or unattractive, or both.

So what does the job actually involve? What sort of people should be thinking about being pastor-teachers? What are its joys and heartaches, and how might some of the practical and conceptual gaps between where you are now and where you might be, be narrowed? Let me mention four important areas.

1. Pastoring and the Word of God

> Now I commit you to God and to the word of his grace, which can build you up and give you an inheritance among all those who are sanctified. **Acts 20 v 32**

In Paul's parting address to the Ephesian elders, he urges them to give themselves to the same work that they have seen him do so effectively among them. His address gives us a number of strong indications of what the work will involve.

In Paul's mind, the pastoring/shepherding role is clearly and explicitly related to teaching. This is particularly evident in Acts 20 v 28-32 where the wolf, the arch-enemy of the shepherd, is one who savages the flock with untruth in order to pursue personal gain.

Christians often use the words 'pastoral' and 'teaching' in inadequate ways. Being 'pastoral' usually means something like 'looking after people in difficulty'; 'teaching' often implies nothing more than the communication of information. Both of these meanings fall far short of their biblical meanings. To pastor God's people is to bring God's Word to bear on their lives in such a way that they are built up together in love, protected and led all the way through this perilous life to a secure and eternal inheritance. Pastoring and teaching are married in the Bible and must never be divorced in ministry.

It is genuinely the case that God's Word does this work in God's people as it is prayerfully applied to life. Yet unless they have deep conviction about this, Christian workers often turn to other means, especially when responsibility grows or circumstances are extreme. I remember being told very early on by an older minister how he had observed Christian leaders losing confidence in the ministry of the Word around the time they themselves became responsible for a congregation—the weight of responsibility and of people's expectations tested their convictions beyond breaking point. When Paul says that an overseer should be 'able to teach' (1 Timothy 3 v 2), he is not talking about technical ability (which is assumed) but about character and conviction. The issue is not so much whether he can teach, but whether he will keep teaching when the pressure is on to do otherwise.

Therefore, the absolute essentials for the role of pastor-teacher are twofold: **conviction** that the ministry of the Word and prayer are the core activities, and some measure of **ability** prayerfully to apply God's Word to one's own life and the lives of others. This combination of living and teaching is powerfully effective in God's hands (1 Timothy 4 v 11-16).

2. Pastoring and the church of God

The work of the pastor-teacher in Acts 20 is a much more diverse, life-engaging and exacting activity than is often imagined. The heart of it is the intimate sharing of life with the congregation. The job involves loving people and leading them, being an example, persuading them of the truth and urging them to live it out together. A couple of related observations might be made here.

First, **loving people is essential.** The work is much more than being a 'Bible teacher'. God's desire is not to see His Word taught, as though His chief interest were hearing the sound of His own voice, but rather that His people should be built up in knowledge, love, unity, and maturity as each part of the body does its work (Ephesians 4 v 11-16). *Pastor teachers need to be 'people' people.* It's not enough to enjoy the Bible, or to enjoy teaching the Bible. One needs to enjoy the sharing of life that goes with it. Acts 20 is full of this,

---

'It's a people job'

Malcolm Jones worked as an accountant for many years and preached widely in Brethren churches around the country in his spare time. This brought home to him the tremendous challenges facing churches without a resident preaching/teaching ministry. Travelling widely, he became aware of great needs within those churches which could not be met by a flying visit; and which, because of the Brethren resistance to full-time ministry, would never be met.

'We eventually moved to a Baptist church, where I became Assistant Pastor for five years, before being invited to be Pastor of a small independent Baptist church. A major problem, initially, was trying to address the stubbornness of some of the older section of the church, who resisted all change from the ancient formats. Helping them to change, in order to reach a new generation of people with the gospel, was distressing at times. Attempts on a one-to-one basis to explain that I wasn't a mad radical who simply liked turning things on their head for the fun of it weren't always successful. Some folk became hostile and some left—but others put their backs into the work for the greater good. Those early experiences were painful to myself and to my family, but have proved to be thoroughly worthwhile.

'This is fundamentally a people job. Pastoring a small church means that there is not a large pool of workers one can train, or to whom one can delegate, and the pressures of organisation and administration easily threaten the time needed to be spent in the Word. I find that the need to rapidly respond to peoples' crises can also be demanding. So I am grateful to those friends and colleagues who understand the biblical priorities, and who do their part in trying to keep me on track.'

as Paul describes how he has lived with the Ephesians, worked with them, urged them and warned them with tears. The Ephesians have not been his audience, but his family. *If you don't love people, don't be a pastor-teacher.*

Second, one often hears discussions between non-conformists and Anglicans about what sort of denominational structure is the best to work in. People argue, often heatedly, about the advantages of their particular 'boat'. Having worked in a variety of boats (Anglican and Free Church) I could now argue fairly convincingly from both sides! But such discussions are fundamentally ill-conceived. They assume, wrongly I think, that any particular boat is going to be adequate for evangelising a diverse nation. More significantly, they assume that differing models of church government really make a difference to the nature of the work of pastoring. This is a great mistake.

The reality is that, no matter what the circumstances, **the task of being a pastor-teacher always involves persuading people of the truth and encouraging them to live it out together.** It always involves encouraging oneself and others to do uncomfortable things together for the sake of the advance of the gospel.

3. Pastoring and protection

Closely allied to the work of teaching truth is that of exposing error (Acts 20 v 28-31, Titus 1 v 9). This is a constant issue in pastoral ministry. Untruth damages people and is usually promoted for the gain of the teacher.

> Ministers must not only be 'pastors', but 'proeliatores' (fighters/ warriors). In one hand they must hold the bread of life and 'feed the flock of God'; in the other hand, they must hold the sword of the Spirit and fight against those errors which carry damnation in their front. **Thomas Watson, *The Beatitudes***

Some caution is required here. It is unhelpful in ministry to develop a love of controversy. It does not lead to congregational health but to an institutional pickiness of a destructive kind. Yet it is vitally important that the pastor-teacher has the stomach for disagreement when necessary, for wolves are common and very dangerous, preying on the weak or immature.

A friend, pastoring a church in continental Europe, mentioned to me once that for the first time in ten years he had felt some peace about going off on holiday. 'Every other year, the minute I have gone away, new people have arrived in church and tried to take it over!'

4. Pastoring and age

Age is an important factor in ministry. Paul is talking to elders (Acts 20 v 17, literally 'older men'). They are referred to as elders for a good reason—they are not 'youngers'. One of the chief reasons that it's hard for young men to imagine themselves in the role of pastor-teacher is that they aren't yet old enough! The Bible expects that, just as older people take responsibility for human families, so those who are older will take responsibility for the household of God. Therefore, it is simply not normal, not in line with how things have been made, for someone in their 20s to feel entirely comfortable about being pastor of a church with a broad age range. This does not mean that 'youngers' are unable to exercise such responsibility, but it is always a difficult thing to do. In fact, Paul instructs Timothy (1 Timothy 4 v 11 – 5 v 2) so that he, very experienced in ministry and probably in early middle-age, will be able to avoid being looked down on because he is 'young'.

My own experience has been that, though I still do not feel particularly 'grown up' or competent, there are many aspects of ministry, particularly things relating to dealing with people, which seem much less terrifying at 45 than they did at 37. No doubt this is, in part, because of a natural growth in experience and conviction, but much of it is simply the product of more birthday celebrations.

So how should someone in their 20s or 30s assess their suitability? The critical question is probably not: can I envisage myself being pastor of a church?, but rather: am I able to exercise a useful ministry among my peers? If you have some ability to exercise a pastoral and teaching ministry among those of your own age, it is likely that greater responsibility for a broader range of people can be shouldered with increasing age.

Putting it all together

So, to sum up:

- *Do you have some ability to teach God's Word and do you enjoy it?*
- *Do you love people?*
- *Are you exercising a useful ministry among your peers that others recognise?*
- *Are you getting older?*

If 'yes' to all the above, then why aren't you thinking about being a pastor-teacher? It's a great ambition in the Bible (1 Timothy 3 v 1)! What's keeping it from being your ambition? What's keeping you from exploring that option further with others? If you are already exploring it then here are some things worth cultivating.

Things worth cultivating

1. Self-education

I am increasingly convinced that the ability to be a perpetual self-educator is pretty much essential for the pastor-teacher. If I am not learning, others are very unlikely to be gripped by what I am teaching. If I am not able to teach myself, I am very unlikely to stay wholeheartedly engaged with the work for three or four decades which is what one should be aiming for.

2. An inquisitive mind

Two of the besetting diseases of pastor-teachers are that they find it hard to listen (because they are always talking), and hard to change their minds (because they are always having to be public about their thoughts). I have found it helpful to cultivate two related attitudes as an antidote to these:

- To assume that I don't understand or believe the passage of the Bible I am studying.

'Living with your mistakes...'

Dick Farr ministers in a rural Anglican parish where he has been for 16 years.

'Although there are many frustrations, there is no other job I would rather be doing. It's a bit like Moses' mother—who was paid by Pharaoh's daughter to look after her own son. I am being set free and supported to do the very thing that I want to do most as a Christian—to see people come to faith, and to grow in their understanding and ability to serve.

'And the job has lots of other advantages: working from home means that I spend more time with my wife and children than most men are able to, and, at least in theory, I have the flexibility to do lots of other things with my time that wouldn't be possible in a normal job.

But the downside is that, because the job is never done, it's easy to not stop working. I'm quite disciplined with days off and holidays, but there is a terrible tendency for work to creep into family life. Being a pastor is different from being a father and husband, and I have to work hard at not mixing the roles up—I'm not always successful.

Staying long-term in a village has its downside too—you have to live with your mistakes! I regularly walk past houses and people that I know I've let down or alienated in some way in the past.

- To assume that I don't know the answer to any question which I am being asked.

I think that my congregation find these refreshing, if bewildering (why doesn't the pastor know?). I certainly find them helpful.

3. A capacity for relationship

It doesn't help to be a shrinking violet in the role of pastor-teacher. It is a great help to be moderately comfortable in the public eye, and to have a fair capacity for relationship. I think that I am naturally at the unhelpful end of this spectrum but a capacity for relationship can be learned with effort.

4. The ability to live with disappointment

When Paul's warning of Acts 20 v 30 turned into reality (which it did, 1 Timothy 1 v 6), it must have been tremendously disappointing. Imagine investing three years in a group of leaders to have some of them turn away from the truth and abuse the church for their own gain. Pastoral ministry involves such disappointments and they need to be endured. The pastor-teacher also has, from time to time, to soak up a few punches for the sake of the congregation. Ultimately, the ability to handle disappointment and absorb hostility comes from theological conviction about the shape of ministry. However, there are temperamental factors which are worth taking into account. If you are naturally a depressive person or very thin skinned, be open-eyed about the fact that measures may need to be put in place to compensate for these things.

5. The ability to live with mediocrity

Most pastor-teachers are not brilliant. Fortunately they don't have to be. The work is about patience, persistence, conviction, hard work, the steady application of pressure in the right direction, the slow grind rather than the quick sprint.

Most pastor-teachers are generalists, and spend quite a bit of time doing things they know others could do better. Many feel that if only they were different then they would be much more useful. If we belong to larger churches we may have leaders whose gifts are significantly greater than average. This can be a great discouragement to someone who feels their gifts are rather ordinary by comparison with others. But this should not discourage you from asking whether the role of pastor-teacher should be pursued.

Pastor-teachers do not have to be clones. You don't have to conform to a particular personality type or skill set. Pastors are like sausages in a delicatessen; they come in all sorts of shapes and sizes; they have all sorts of personalities, skills and temperaments. Different individuals are suited for different situations. The core work and convictions are the same, but these are expressed in a wide diversity of contexts. It is important that this is embraced seriously by anyone thinking about pastoral ministry. We do not have to be the same or like our leaders in terms of richness of gifts.

The responsibility is magnificent

Finally, let me say, there is nothing like it. It is challenging and stretching in almost every way. There is always more to learn and more to do. It is never boring. The privilege of sharing life with others is exceptional. More than this, and most importantly, the Lord Jesus will reap for Himself a great harvest from the work of His Word. This puts the whole into perspective. There are many, many attractions about all sorts of work in this world. There are things which confer more immediate reward, a greater sense of satisfaction or fulfillment, but there is nothing quite like this which will, in Jesus' hands, endure for ever.

The realities of being an evangelist!

By Roger Carswell

EVANGELISM IS PROCLAIMING THE GOSPEL to non-Christians, who are listening. The Bible places its emphasis on the message rather than the method, on the *evangel* rather than the way we are to *evangel-ise*. I sometimes hear it said that every Christian is an evangelist. This is not strictly true. Every Christian is a witness, demonstrating by words and works the significance of Christ and Him crucified. Pastors, through the instruction given to Timothy, are told to do the work of the evangelist. However, according to Ephesians 4 v 11, there are those whose supreme gifting and calling is to be an evangelist. If he, or she, is distracted into other priorities, there will inevitably be a sense of frustration, and lack of joy in service.

I fear that the church has been neglectful in that it has not looked for, encouraged and used people with evangelistic gifting. Colleges have often shifted the evangelist into pastoral or Bible teaching ministry. Today, with so much spiritual ignorance, the need for people to be set aside to give themselves primarily to evangelism, is overwhelming. Churches have pastors, assistant pastors, youth workers. administrators, and praise God for them all, but where are the evangelists who will work with those outside the church, faithfully introducing them to Jesus?

Our wonderful message

Evangelism is not 'Christianising' (i.e. gradually influencing people towards a Christian conviction), but the proclamation of the gospel, explaining who God is, and who we are; what God has done, and what we must do. The apostle Paul wrote: 'I resolved to know nothing while I was with you, except Jesus Christ and him crucified' (1 Corinthians 2 v 2). His message was of a definite Christ, and a definite crucifixion, with all its significance. That led to the definite conclusion that the person and work of Christ were to be the overriding themes of Paul's preaching, and in turn, of every evangelist. There are at least fourteen completely different settings in the book of Acts, where Paul preached. He didn't merely evangelise his friends; people who were a million miles from the things of God heard the gospel, and were converted.

'I want to work for Jesus'

When John became a Christian as a child of seven, he was asked by a school friend what he wanted to do when he grew up. 'I want to work for Jesus!' he replied. A desire that eventually led him to work with the London City Mission.

'I started by working as a probationer, helping run a mission centre in Battersea, South London, which I eventually went on to lead. More recently I have taken up a post attached to an Anglican parish in North London as a church-based evangelist. My primary focus is to reach out by doing door-to-door work in the area. It's very hard work; a bit like diamond mining, you have to hack your way through a lot of coal before you come across the real prize—the one that God has chosen. I only do a limited amount of preaching and teaching—most of my work is one-to-one.

'I just love meeting people and going into their homes, and getting involved in their lives in the right kind of way. In the last week I have had three men break down in front of me—each of them is going through a very difficult time. There's a great privilege of sharing burdens with people—offering practical support—and building the bridges that will allow me to share the good news with them at the right moment.'

With such a glorious message, the evangelist will want to create and take every opportunity to ensure that unconverted people are hearing it. It is not a nine-to-five task, but a consuming passion. It is our life's greatest work. It is not sufficient to go through the routine of preaching; there must be an attempt to ensure that unconverted people are hearing, and, as much as we are able to bring this about, are understanding of what is being said. So the evangelist will try to ensure that his or her vocabulary and manner are both becoming, and relevant, to the listeners. The apostle Peter was supposed to be the one who caught the ear of the listener; instead he cut off the ear of the High Priest's servant! Too many have followed his bad example.

Evangelists will seek every legitimate opportunity to proclaim the good news of Jesus to lost men and women. They will always strive to get the Bible message into the minds of people. Nothing will thrill an evangelist more than being able to explain the simplicity of the gospel to either an individual or to a crowd. It will pain an evangelist to be in a situation where the gospel is not being proclaimed with a sense of clarity and urgency. Evangelists should not be abrasive, nor go out of their way to provoke trouble, but will want to winsomely and faithfully present the claims of Christ to those who listen. However, the message is such that, if presented faithfully, it would lead to them being put out of a synagogue, mosque or temple, as happened so often to the early believers in Acts.

Trials and triumphs

In 2 Corinthians 4 v 8-9 and 6 v 8-10 Paul, writing autobiographically, gives *thirteen* contrasting views of his work, which was primarily that of a gospel preacher. God had shown Paul at his conversion how many things he would have to suffer for the name of

Jesus (Acts 9 v 16), and now Paul is writing his own confirmation of the Lord's word. He is describing the trials and triumphs of being an evangelist. He is speaking the language of experience.

I remember sitting in a street café in Maastricht, chatting and drinking coffee with my daughter. On the next table to us was a black family. Then walking along the street, as is the Dutch custom, came a newly married couple. Everyone around was standing and applauding. The bride in her white gown was beautiful, tall, blonde and white. Her new husband was handsome, smart, tall and black. I mischievously remarked, 'Lucky guy!' The black lady next to me turned and said, 'Lucky girl!' We were both right, but were seeing things from different viewpoints. I had seen the white woman, she had seen the black man! When Paul describes what it has meant to be an evangelist, he looks at it all from two points of view, both right, but very different.

Paul had already spoken of his troubles, hardships and distresses, as he had compared himself with the intruding minister in Corinth. Now he contrasts his own weakness with God's power. The Christian always knows both 'crucifixion' and a 'resurrection'. All that Paul describes about himself, the Lord has experienced in His suffering in a far greater way.

There is a price to be paid, and there are blessings to be received. James Denney wrote: 'God will always have His work done by instruments who are willing to have it clear that the exceeding greatness of the power is His, and not theirs.'

There are thirteen contrasts, but I have grouped them into four sections of hardship:

1. Physical hardship: the body is persecuted, but it is not destroyed.

Paul outlines some of the ways his body has suffered as a conse-

quence of his devotion to getting the message of the gospel to all.
He says he has been:

- persecuted, but not abandoned (4 v 9)
- struck down, but not destroyed (4 v 9). Moffat translates this:
  'knocked down, but not knocked out'
- dying, and yet we live on (6 v 9)
- chastened, and yet not killed (6 v 9)

He suffered terrible pressure from those outside of Christ—blow
after blow, but they were not fatal. All the weight of suffering did
not extinguish in him the joys of the new life he had in Christ,
and the special privilege of the ministry. In 2 Corinthians 11 he
lists what his body went through, but for him they were the marks
of authenticity in his calling. He was not one who lived 'on flow-
ery beds of ease'. There will be times when we too feel utterly
exhausted, and unable to keep going in the work. As a travelling
evangelist, I spend hundreds of hours driving on motorways,
when all sensible people are in bed! The only regular thing about
my life is its irregularity, and eventually your body pays a price for
that lifestyle. In such times we know that the Lord, who Himself
experienced exhaustion, is able to renew our strength, to enable us
to mount up with wings as eagles, to run and not faint and to walk
and not grow weary. Walking is the hardest of those!

2. Emotional hardship: the mind at a loss or the
spirit cast down, but never despairing.

Paul says he was:

- perplexed, but not in despair (4 v 9)
- sorrowful, yet always rejoicing (6 v 10)

There was an irrepressible fountain of grace within him. For the
evangelist, there is always a sense of sadness at the lostness of the
lost. It is the 'fellowship of Christ's sufferings'. There can be real

inward hurt and pain concerning those who are unconverted. And yet, there is deep joy when people are being saved. Many have known what it is to actually, while sleeping, dream about the lost, as well as to pray that they would be saved. It is a burden that the god of this age has blinded them.

Then, Paul knew the disappointment concerning backsliders—those who showed initial signs of genuine faith after professing conversion, but didn't go on with the Lord. There was grief too, and great sadness, at lack of integrity in Christians. It hurts when Christians, who should know better, by their bad behaviour cause

---

Keeping fresh...

Pete worked as an itinerant evangelist for 20 years but now pastors a small church. 'I loved the variety of being an evangelist. You get into loads of situations which are just out of the ordinary. I've spoken at a Freemasons lodge, where there was an incredible sense of evil. I've spoken in pubs to blokes who looked like they would rather beat me up than listen. I took it as a challenge to get them to listen.

'I still do a lot of travelling around, but these days, I am much more church based. The biggest problem in being an itinerant is that you don't see follow up. If you're travelling around it's difficult to be properly connected to a church. You've got to be part of a supportive fellowship to keep you real, and to keep you from getting lazy or discouraged. There's a temptation to just do the same few talks that you know are good—but then the danger is that you get stale and preach without conviction, and you end up not growing yourself. It's a real effort to keep pushing yourself in the Bible to discover the richness of the gospel, and new angles on presenting it.

'I also need to know the world. Some people are so 'in the Word', they seem to live in the first century—not living today. I want to help Christians know how to attack the world—not just defend the gospel. So I 'people watch' over coffee in the town centre. I read biographies, and discuss them with the guys I am encouraging. I watch films and read novels—all the time asking myself: 'what is this telling me about the modern mindset—and how is that an opportunity for the gospel?'

the enemies of God to blaspheme His name. Others weaken the gospel by failing to proclaim it fully and faithfully. All this hurts, but it is to be surpassed by the joy of knowing and walking with God.

The mind may be at a loss, but it is not utterly lost: there are people who are being saved and are making great progress in the Lord.

I have in my study a copy of Rembrandt's great painting of Jeremiah weeping over Jerusalem when it was being destroyed. He, like Jesus, was a man of sorrows, and evangelists will experience that sorrow too.

Dear Lord, I ask for the eyes that see
Deep down to the world's sore need
I ask for a love that holds not back
But pours out itself indeed.
I want the passionate power of prayer
That yearns for the great crowd's soul;
I want to go 'mongst the fainting sheep
And tell them my Lord makes whole.

Let me look at the crowd as my Saviour did
'Til my eyes with tears grow dim;
Let me look 'til I pity the wandering sheep
And love them for love of Him.

3. Social hardship: socially an outcast, but never deserted

The apostle Paul also draws our attention to the social cost that is involved in prioritising gospel work and evangelism. His says his life has been characterised by paradoxical tensions:

- By honour and dishonour (6 v 8)
- By evil report and good report (6 v 8)

- As deceivers and yet true (6 v 8)
- As unknown and yet well known (ie: no standing in the world) (6 v 9)

Though Paul was in some places esteemed by Christians, he also experienced times of extreme loneliness. The centre of his activity was with people who were critical and scathing not only of his message, but also of him. Like his Master, hounded by those who wanted to get rid of the new religion, Paul was under terrible pressure. And yet escaping that pressure he could rest in the intimate relationship with Jesus which he enjoyed.

The world still shows its best and worst to those who proclaim Christ. Its reverence, affection and praise are sometimes poured on gospel workers in recognition that they are spreading kindness and compassion in a hurting world. But its hatred, indifference and scorn are also showered on those who preach Jesus, the Sacrifice, Substitute and only Saviour of the world. It can be hard to stand up in a university refectory, or even a school assembly, to share the gospel, and in effect be frozen by the glares that are making it obvious that people don't want to hear what you have to say.

When evangelism is the passion of your work, even some Christians will make it clear that your message is not popular. For the evangelist, and particularly the travelling evangelist, there will be times of extreme loneliness. There is a separation from family, and even from one's local church. When my wife and I celebrated our silver wedding anniversary, we organised an evangelistic meal for friends and family. I remember my wife whispering part-way through the event, 'This is fraudulent: we've only had six years together!' She wasn't grumbling (she never has) but there was truth in what she said, and it underlined the importance of partnership in ministry.

To recognise the eternal plight of unconverted people leads the evangelist to devote time, energy and resources to making Jesus known to the lost world. Indelibly etched on my mind are the challenging words of John Wesley: 'Leisure and I have parted.' That means that there is a price to be paid, which the marriage and the family pay, and times of loneliness for those who are single, as well as those with a family. But Jesus said: 'If anyone comes to me and does not hate his father and mother, his wife and children, his brothers and sisters—yes, even his own life—he cannot be my disciple. And anyone who does not carry his cross and follow me cannot be my disciple.' (Luke 14 v 26-27). Of course, the evangelist has responsibilities towards his family, so there is great wisdom needed, that will vary according to each individual, as to how every hour is used for the glory of God.

Jesus 'made Himself of no reputation' (Philippians 2 v 7 NKJV), so who are we to grasp after the very thing Jesus has renounced? The saintly Scottish minister Robert Murray McCheyne said: 'I see a man cannot be a faithful minister until he preaches Christ for Christ's sake.' We serve the Lord here on earth, knowing that there is coming a day when we will share with Him in heaven.

4. Material hardship: materially poor, but never destitute

Paul knew real deprivation of things and luxuries:

- hard pressed on every side, but not crushed (4 v 8)
- As having nothing, and yet possessing everything (6 v 10)
- As poor, yet making many rich (6 v 10)

Living by faith reminds me of the man who jumped off a tower block. As he passed the 15th floor, he shouted to someone inside the building, 'I'm alright so far!' There are times in evangelistic work when one is abused. I have found that often those who can afford to cover your expenses don't, while others who can't afford it, do! Again though, like the incident in Maastricht, it depends on one's focus. Times of abuse? Yes, there have been many. However, there are other times when people have been overwhelmingly generous. I have had occasions of remarkable provision that can only lead one to recognise and thank God for His kindness.

Evangelists who are honouring the Lord with their resources are not going to be rich, but they will have the immense joy of using the resources at their disposal to minister to others.

After describing the vivid range of his experiences, Paul concludes with a victorious spirit. Seeing that death was at work in him, Paul knew that life was at work in those with whom he shared. (2 Corinthians 4 v 12). God does not waste any of our tears, pain or sacrifice. By the Lord's grace, I need not be moved by any of these.

Jesus experienced hardship in the same areas:

- **Physically:** He died on the cross carrying our sins and judgement on Himself.
- **Emotionally**: moved with compassion at lost cities and citizens.
- **Socially:** friends who once forsook everything to follow Him, forsook Him and fled.
- **Materially:** He had nothing—nowhere to sleep or even lay His head.

And yet, through His death, rising again and exaltation, what riches are His! He has a blood-bought church, which revels in His grace and goodness. Our Lord Jesus gave His all to us, and means so much, that to devote our lives to making Him known, either as a witness, doing the work of an evangelist, or as an evangelist, surely is our spiritual act of worship.

I, for one, wouldn't want to do anything else, and feel immensely privileged to speak about Jesus to anyone who will listen.

Church planters for the harvest field

Tim Chester

I SEE IT IN THEIR EYES AND I HEAR IT IN THEIR VOICES. It is mainly pity, but there is also a hint of respect, even admiration. The leader of an established congregation will be asking me how things are going. It is clear they regard church planting as some kind of extreme sport. Church planters are doing the ministry equivalent of hang-gliding or rock climbing.

A church-planting friend of mine was once speaking on the subject. His host gave a long introduction, emphasising what hard work church planting was; how demanding and dangerous. When my friend was finally allowed to speak he said: 'Sorry to disabuse you, but church planting is easy. The difficult task was done by a man on a cross 2,000 years ago.' Yet, church planting is hard work; it has its disappointments, its frustrations and its anxieties. So does all gospel ministry. After all, the cross is the model for Christian living. But Jesus is the Saviour of the world—not church planters. He is the hero—not me. He is the One who will build His church. My role is simply to proclaim His finished work.

Church planting is not for would-be heroes who want to cover themselves in glory. It is not for people who want to prove themselves before they move onto bigger and better things. It is for people who believe the gospel; who will do ministry in confident dependence on Christ's work and the Spirit's power.

I deserve neither more pity nor more respect than anyone else engaged in gospel ministry. It is tempting to bask in the *kudos* of being an 'on the edge' church planter, but I would not swap places with my ministerial friends in traditional churches. The truth is I pity them!

The advantages of being small...

When Richard graduated from theological college, he was asked to lead a group of 25 people from an existing congregation to plant a new evening congregation in Balham, south London.

'When I first started the process that led to me being in full-time ministry, I had no idea that I would be involved in church planting. I'm not sure I even knew what it was! During my time as an apprentice I had been part of a mini church plant but it was a complete disaster. I learned some valuable lessons.

'When we launched in Balham as a evening congregation, we didn't really have much more than the people, a Bible and a place to meet. We're now four years old and under God we have grown by about ten people each year. We also launched a morning congregation a year ago. If we're honest, our growth has occurred through transfer, biological (ie: babies being born) and only modest evangelistic growth. My biggest frustration is that we've seen so few conversions, despite having good numbers of people coming to evangelistic events and going through our evangelistic courses.

'If we're too ambitious when we're few in numbers we can make too many demands on a core of enthusiastic and active members and we all end up completely exhausted. We need real wisdom to know what to say 'no' to.

'But being small has some great advantages. I love the quality of personal relationships. We notice when people are missing, and I find that I know more about what's going on in people's lives.

'Church planting seems to have taken on a whole ministry genre of its own, but in reality it's not that different from what many ministers do week by week. Everything we do is built around Bible teaching, prayer, evangelism, and encouragement in personal godliness. That's at the heart of what we've tried to do.'

Mission rather than maintenance

Many of their battles are often about repairing the church building, restructuring the programme, placating the malcontents. My battles are all about finding a home for a destitute refugee, believing the gospel when your boss bullies you, turning from a life of sexual promiscuity to follow Christ. My battles are all about faith and repentance. Of course, ministers in established churches have those battles too. But they have other distractions as well. They have to negotiate rotas, committee meetings, music styles, and the endless details that can consume a pastor's time.

Mission very easily becomes one activity in church life among others. Over time, churches seem to acquire committees, meetings, programmes, traditions. None of these may be wrong in themselves, but cumulatively, they can move the church from mission mode to maintenance mode. Time and energy is spent running the institution.

The great thing about church planting is that it inevitably and naturally shifts the church into missionary mode. It ensures that mission defines the nature, purpose and activity of the church. In a well-established church of a hundred, there is a natural tendency to do what you did last year and for many in the congregation to become passengers. When there are ten of you starting out afresh, everything is evaluated in the light of your mission and everyone is engaged in that mission. And that is so much more exciting.

Community rather than performance

Perhaps people pity me teaching the Bible to a small group instead of preaching to a large congregation. But I love wrestling with a passage together as a community. It is exhilarating to see the Word shaping lives week by week, and not only individual lives, but the life of the Christian community as a whole. Unbelievers asking questions of the text, and believers wanting to know how it applies to specific situations—this is how I have learnt most from God's Word. Pulpit preaching may reach many more, but has a number of drawbacks. The Word goes forth, but there is little opportunity for feedback, no clarification can be given and any application must be at the most general level.

Sermons can easily become a performance art. Conference speakers set the standard, and we listeners become adept at rating them. The pressure on ministers to perform is huge. There is no room for a bad week. Some people seem to think the ability to evaluate sermons is a mark of godliness. But the true mark of godliness is to tremble at God's Word (Isaiah 66 v 2). James says: 'Do not merely listen to the Word, and so deceive yourselves. Do what it says.' (James 1 v 22) Speaking and listening to the Word is a measure of nothing. What counts is *doing* the Word. What I love about church planting is that it creates a context in which it is natural to be Word-centred all through the week; not just for half an hour on a Sunday morning. We exhort, rebuke and comfort one another with the gospel 'every day' (Hebrews 3 v 13). We make decisions—individual decisions and corporate decisions—as a community seeking to be shaped by God's Word.

Team rather than professionalism

Many of my ministerial friends are lonely or they lack companions. However much they work against it, there is a measure of professional distance between them and their congregations. Some people even cultivate this. Church planting, by contrast, removes the distinction between clergy and laity. When you have ten people discussing how they can plant a church together, you inevitably have a gospel team. In church planting, everyone is involved in the ministry—whether they have a full-time secular job, part-time work or are funded in some other way. We form a team of gospel partners, working together to plant the church. The language of 'you' ('you should do this', 'you have done well') is replaced by the language of 'we' ('we should do this', 'we have done well'). There is a sense of ownership and companionship. We celebrate gospel fruit together and we share our discouragements together. The experience of a team is one I would not swap for any sort of pedestal, be it ever so high.

Someone was telling me recently about the number of churches in their denomination without 'pastors'. They were bemoaning the fact that so few young men have the commitment to go 'into the ministry'. We have lots of young people interested in church planting, I thought to myself, with a passion for Christ and a maturity far beyond anything I had at their age. We have people in their mid-twenties leading churches. There are plenty of young Christians today with commitment to Christ. But they do not want to be the omni-competent minister, leading churches on their own. They want to be part of a team, partnering with gospel companions. And this is how it is in church planting.

Brokenness rather than respectability

Church planting is also very messy. This is not church for churched people or respectable people. This is church for the unchurched. This is church for broken people—for 'the poor in spirit' as Jesus calls them (Matthew 5 v 3). This is church for people with messed-up lives. Little is hidden and nothing is sanitised. For every two steps forward you take with people, you also take one, two or even three steps back. But who would have it any other way? Who wants sanitised church? Not those who follow the One who said: 'It is not the healthy who need a doctor, but the sick. I have not come to call the righteous, but sinners' (Mark 2 v

17). Not those who follow the 'friend of sinners' (Luke 7 v 34).

Moreover, it is as part of a community of messy, broken people that I have been able to confront the brokenness in my own life. I am being set free from sins that have held me captive for years. Here is a community in which I can be real. I do not have to perform or pretend. I can be honest, and so find the encouragement and accountability I need to overcome sin. It can be painful. But I would not want to return to mere attendance, hiding away in a large congregation. I no longer need to hide. I am accepted as a sinner by a community of people who model God's grace to me and who are committed to my transformation by that grace.

'Our biggest surprise: it's possible! '

Andrew became a Christian in his first year at university. He joined UCCF as a Relay worker for a couple of years, and then, after working for a secular charity for two years, joined UCCF again as a staff worker in Liverpool.

'There was a desperate need for a Bible-teaching church in the centre of Liverpool, and my colleagues and I were always pleading with people to come and start something. Then at a conference someone said to us: 'The cavalry will never come—do it yourself.' After some consultation with local churches we decided to go ahead with a team of 15 people—contacts from the CU work, and a few people who were prepared to move into the area. Christ Church Liverpool was born.

My biggest surprise was that it was actually possible! I think we had read one book between us on church planting. We discovered that church planting is not really that complicated, but the job of running things each week is really hard work. We had no building, so we had to transport stuff all over the place. Nor was there much stability—we didn't know who would come each week. I was constantly on edge about it all the time. We had good external support, and stable finances, so there was a lot going for us. Even so, after a year, I was exhausted. So we have now deliberately increased the number of people involved: elders, deacons, ministry trainees, and we've just appointed another pastor.'

Church planting has brought me so many blessings. So even if you do not become one, there is no need to pity us and no reason to admire us either.

Preaching the gospel where Christ is not known

But I am not committed to church planting simply because of its benefits to me. I am an advocate of church planting because I am convinced this is the best way to win people for Christ. Apostolic mission was church planting. Paul planted churches wherever he went on his missionary journeys. Christian mission cannot be divorced from Christian community. The Christian community is an illustration of the gospel. People see the transforming power of grace as they observe our relationships (John 13 v 34-35; 17 v 20-23). The God who cannot be seen lives in us as we love one another (1 John 4 v 12). And Paul planted churches because individuals are discipled as part of Christian communities. It is in the church that we see gospel living modelled across generations. It is in the church that we find people who will encourage, teach and challenge us to walk in a way worthy of the calling we have received. This is not some idealised version of church. It is in the day-to-day interaction of the local church with its awkward customers, contrasting generations and conflicting personalities that my selfishness and laziness are exposed. This is where I learn to deny myself and take up my cross.

There are many areas of our country, and countries in our world where there is no gospel witness. There are many areas where churches do exist, but which nevertheless contain people who are not being reached with the gospel. These communities will only be reached if we plant churches. They will only be reached if we plant churches that go on and plant more churches. We do not just need church plants; we need church plants planting churches. We need to plant churches with church planting in their DNA.

Church planting is a great opportunity to contextualise the gospel afresh to reach people who are not currently being reached by established churches. As things stand, traditional churches are reaching 10-20 per cent of the population. Church planting is an opportunity to ask whether the way we do church is true to the Bible and true to our context. There is much talk about 'new ways of being church', 'emerging church' and 'new expressions of church'. Some of this reflects a postmodern culture that downplays truth; some reflects a 'me-centred' culture which wants a form of church that indulges my selfish desires.

We need churches that address this culture without capitulating to it. We need gospel-centred churches. The gospel is a word and so we need churches shaped by God's Word rather than by tradition or culture. And the gospel is a missionary word so we need churches geared towards mission that contextualises the gospel for our contemporary world. Church planting is an opportunity to renew the church.

We need to be taking risks and therefore also accepting failure. We need to redefine success away from church as a professionally-run preaching centre with fancy graphics, polished performances and large audiences. We need to define success as Jesus did: broken people hearing the good news (Matthew 5 v 3). We need to define success as Paul did: churches of weak and marginalised people being planted through the message of Christ crucified (1 Corinthians 1 v 18-31). We need people who share Paul's ambition to preach the gospel where Christ is not known, rather than people who aspire to 'inherit' large, established congregations (Romans 15 v 20).

Gospel ministry overseas

Andy Lines

> After this I looked, and behold, a great multitude that no one
> could number, from every nation, from all tribes and peoples and
> languages, standing before the throne and before the Lamb,
> clothed in white robes, with palm branches in their hands, and
> crying out with a loud voice, 'Salvation belongs to our God who
> sits on the throne, and to the Lamb!' And all the angels were
> standing around the throne and worshipped God, saying 'Amen!
> Blessing and glory and wisdom and thanksgiving and honour
> and power and might be to our God for ever and ever! Amen.'"
>
> **Revelation 7 v 9-12**

This is one of the pictures of the new creation in Revelation. To
this end, God is working His purposes out 'as year succeeds to
year'. This is the end that God has had in mind from the beginning. The whole Bible oozes with what God has done in order to
bring this about. We live in the 'last days', after the suffering and
resurrection of the Christ (Luke 24 v 46), and before His coming
again, when God will bring all this to final completion. We live in
the times when repentance and forgiveness of sins should be proclaimed in His name to all nations, beginning from Jerusalem
(Luke 24 v 47).

What a wonderful sight that great multitude will be—there is no
way that it will be a monochrome experience! As, however, we
look at the world around us, we can see the enormity of the task.
With a current world population of around 6 billion souls, even a

conservative estimate will show that some 4 billion are not yet 'clothed with white robes', and are therefore unprepared to face the Lord Jesus when He comes to judge, and so they face an eternity 'shut out from the presence of the Lord' (2 Thess 1 v 9).

So God has clearly made known His will that many from all nations, tribes, peoples and languages will make up His rescued people. He has done everything necessary for this to come about in the death, resurrection and ascension of Jesus, and the pouring out of the Holy Spirit. How can His rescued people not engage in His mission of proclaiming the gospel until He comes again?

There is huge need in our own country to make Christ known. But in God's sovereign purposes, we live in a country where millions from other nations are coming to study or live, and we must take every opportunity to ensure that they too hear the gospel. But the Lord does not allow us to think that, if we have done all this, then we have then done what He requires. Because there yet remain the billions overseas who have never heard the good news. It is not our responsibility to guarantee the right response but it is our responsibility to ensure that they hear. This chapter deals briefly with how you, as a Christian, should and could be part of God's worldwide mission, whether by going yourself in some capacity or supporting those who go.

When I was a soldier in a tank regiment, each year would bring new, improved equipment to help us do our job better. It usually came in the form of 'bolt-on' boxes, somehow fitted into the already cramped turret, and which we then had to avoid damaging with our boots or bashing our heads against. While these boxes often made life easier, we constantly had to practise what were called 'reversionary modes', which meant procedures and drills to be employed in the event that one particular box of tricks failed to work. Sometimes I get the impression that churches treat world mission as a 'bolt-on' extra—something you can opt into if you happen to like travel or have some other related interest, but not an obligation for all Christians. God does not think world mission is an optional extra and neither should His people.

What does it involve?

While we probably still tend to think of world mission (if we think of it at all), in Victorian stereotypical ways, as being done largely by white Westerners, leaving the West, to go and live for the rest of their lives, in some remote and undeveloped part of the world, that would neither reflect current realities, nor suggest an ideal future scenario:

- **The workforce.** The centre of gravity of global Christianity is moving southwards and eastwards (the median is moving through Mali to Northern Nigeria at 17km per annum). Thus the workforce engaged in His mission is also increasingly non-Western (and non-white), and countries such as South Korea, Singapore, India, Nigeria and Brazil are increasingly to the fore.

- **The need.** With Western countries largely representing a spiritual wilderness, the need for mission is at least as much in the West as in other parts of the world, and so mission workers are coming into the West as well as leaving it.

- **The timescale.** There is no doubt that communicating Christ across cultural boundaries is not something that can be done quickly or easily. God's mission desperately needs people willing to give a lifetime of service to the task, but, increasingly, there are opportunities for others willing and able to give shorter periods of time whether as young people, or as those taking career breaks, early or normal retirement; or those who offer their gifts and experience for a few weeks a year. While the opportunities for short-term mission are indeed growing, we should not fall into the trap of overestimating what can be achieved in the short term (nor of underestimating what can be achieved in the long term).

- **The context.** Many mission partners are living and working in poor and undeveloped areas at great personal cost; for the average Westerner the lifestyle gap between what they leave behind and what they encounter overseas is growing. We still need to remember, however, that even the rich and materially well-endowed people around the world also need the gospel. Geographically, Europe is one of the biggest challenges for global mission.

- **The resources.** Although 70-80% of global Christians are now from the global south and therefore the major part of God's

Training leaders in Paris

Ed and Laura work in Paris as student workers attached to IFES (The International Federation of Evangelical Students). They had initially gone as team members, but after a year Ed was made team leader.

'It's a great experience of the French evangelical world,' said Laura. 'All the denominations we know in France are desperate for pastors because the French Christians seem so reluctant to go forward for full-time ministry. I think that's partly because there is so little good, regular Bible teaching going on here.

'Because of the Catholic background that most people have here, French students are often quite up for talking about faith, and even for reading the Bible one to one. The opportunities are enormous, but our focus has been more on trying to develop French Christian students in their own discipleship. One of the most exciting things that Ed has done is to start a preachers' club for mature students and young graduates. They meet every month, for training and to critique each other's work. Three men from the programme have just started at theological college.' Ed and Laura hope to move on to church planting work in Paris at some stage in the future.

workforce, Christians in the Western churches still have a huge amount to offer: more than 80% of church financial resources are located in Western churches. Less easy to measure is the fruit of years of Bible ministry: my experience is that most churches in the south still long to have some of the biblical teaching and training available through lively gospel churches in this country.

What I am saying is this: we need to be thinking how to use our abundance of resources in people, experience and finances for the cause of God's global mission. That will mean opening our eyes to such things as resourcing mission from the poorer countries, even with all the difficulties of such things as accountability. For the cost of a Western single or married mission partner, often with years of expensive training before they become effective, and often serving in that capacity for a short time (up to 5 years would not be untypical), dozens of mission workers from southern continents could be funded, people who are often willing to give a lifetime of service.

With all that I have said above, however, there is no excuse for Western Christians not to get personally involved, in the short or long term. As Paul says in 1 Corinthians 9 v 23: 'I do it all [gives up all his rights] for the sake of the gospel, *that I may share with them in its blessings'* (ESV, my emphasis). There is a surprise here, for we would expect Paul to say that he sacrificed his rights for the sake of the gospel so that they (his hearers) would share in *its* blessings; instead Paul says that it is so that he and they would share in its blessings. There is simply no other way to be a Christian than to surrender our rights and be prepared to go anywhere for the sake of the gospel, for that was the way of the Saviour.

What I am saying here though, is that we need to think very carefully before we take up any opportunity for gospel ministry overseas, to ensure that our deployment is the best way of furthering the gospel cause, because it may well be that there are others who could and would do it better if given the opportunity; just because Western churches have so much of the resources available does not mean that they have to be used to resource only Westerners engaged in global mission. This kind of thinking, to ensure that we are not being strategically naïve, is best done in the context of the local church that knows us best, and perhaps in conjunction with a world mission agency that may have more objective knowledge of the international scene.

'I saw the greater need...'

When Mike was studying for a business degree, he began to work with international students, encouraged by an older Christian who was discipling him. He ended up sharing a flat with an Iranian and a Lebanese student, and got his first real taste of trying to communicate the gospel with people from another culture. After college, Mike worked first in the government tax office and then in sports-ground management before his first ministry job as a youth pastor in a Baptist church.

'I read one day the statistic that 94% of the world's Christian ministers were working with just 6% of the world's population, and I liked the idea of trying to reach people in these under-served areas. My background was with Spanish speaking people and with muslims—so southern Spain seemed to be the most obvious place to go, where I could use my experience.

'While I was there, I met my wife who is Egyptian. I had already visited Morocco several times, and saw the need to go where the need was even greater. When Safaa and I got married, we had to make a choice: would I move into the Arab world, or would she join me in the Spanish world? We decided to go to Morocco; and the mission agency that was supporting Safaa agreed to take us both on.

'To anyone considering overseas mission, I always encourage them to make a visit, and to ask the question: "Could I live here?" The younger you are when you start, the more flexible you tend to be, and, of course, it's easier to learn a new language.'

The Cost

This points us towards a very important truth for all those involved in gospel ministry, whether here or overseas: it will be costly.

If we are to engage in gospel ministry cross-culturally, we will face the costs of all gospel ministry (reputation, ridicule, opposition, heartache, weariness and so on), but we will also face additional costs:

- **Learning a new language and culture.** Some are naturally (and very irritatingly!) gifted in their ability to pick up other languages and some work in areas where English is the common medium, but there are really no short-cuts to learning another culture in order to be able to communicate Christ. For most Westerners it is a humbling (and sanctifying and therefore good) experience to be reduced to being a cultural baby again; where how you speak, dress, sit, look, walk, queue, ask, show appreciation, play sport, eat, sleep, argue and generally live are all things to be learned from scratch, and usually done under the bemused gaze of those whose culture you are trying to learn. Worse still can be the experience of having to work alongside other motivated Westerners, who may share much in common with us, and may even speak our language fluently, but whose way of doing things is surprisingly different. We expect cultural differences with most others but are often caught unawares by differences with those who 'should' be like us.

- **Distance from loved ones.** Although there are now numerous ways of keeping in touch with friends and family, and cheap air travel means that trips back are more feasible and frequent, there is no escaping the issue of separation. The cost of immersing yourself in, and adapting to, another culture inevitably means distancing yourself from your own. Many feel depressed and bewildered that their loved ones have 'moved on' in the interim, and they find they have less in common. Another cost in this area is the shallowness and brevity of interest shown in the experience that you have gained by people of your own culture: the eyes can glaze over remarkably quickly when you begin to tell of your experiences or, worse, show any photos!

- **Carrying out subservient roles.** In the not-too-distant past, Western missionaries were at the forefront of world mission

---

'The need for training is desperate...'

Mark trained for the Anglican ministry at Ridley Hall, Cambridge, where he did an MA. 'I met my wife Rachel at Cornhill. She had been born in Uganda and lived in East Africa for most of her childhood. At Cornhill I also became close friends with an African student. The church we worked at after training had a very strong tradition of supporting overseas mission, so it was the most natural thing to think about going.

'We visited Uganda five times before we moved there. I had already begun to know my way round Kampala, and saw the real needs that were there. There was no great 'Damascus Road' experience, just the rather mundane realisation that we were there and we could help. Once we decided to offer our help things slotted into place quite quickly.'

Mark went to teach at the Kampala Evangelical School of Theology (KEST), where he did a variety of jobs over the four years he worked there. 'There is a huge need for training in Africa. They don't really need evangelists or teachers—they've got the personnel—but they desperately need training. There is room in Uganda for at least another 20 colleges like KEST!'

Mark has returned to the UK to work in a London church, but will be involved in travelling overseas with the Langham Partnership for six weeks each year, running preaching conferences. But the door has not closed on living and working overseas again. 'When you've made the move once, you know you can do it again—so the thought of moving overseas is not so intimidating,' he said.

---

endeavours as pioneers, and then as leaders of new churches. There are still many opportunities for pioneering in new situations. There are also many roles for which, on paper, Western mission workers are well equipped. There were few in Latin America who had had the privileged preparation and training that I had received, and they were used to highly qualified and motivated Westerners coming and giving the leadership that they themselves had no hope of competing with. Yet is it right that, by virtue of our privileged background, we assume positions of leadership in national churches? Modern Western mission partners need to have a clear idea that they are going to serve under national leaders, even if less highly qualified than they are themselves. This can be a hugely frustrating experience but again one which is very good for us, and for the worldwide church of Christ.

- **Loss of career and family prospects.** While it could be argued that a time of service overseas is excellent experience for a variety of roles in Britain, not all potential employers will see things like that. They may focus more on the fact that you have not followed a more normal career path and have in effect become de-skilled. At the same time, for some, possibilities of marriage are reduced in an overseas setting; for others who are married and have children there are agonising decisions about schooling and questions such as: which culture do my children belong to?

Of course, with these potential sacrifices for the gospel come many huge compensations 'in this present age' (Mark 10 v 30), such as being part of the multicultural body that is the church, in ways that we may not experience in our own culture unless we happen to attend a rare, mixed congregation. Another incentive that I found in Latin America, but which is not necessarily replicated elsewhere, is the overt and genuine interest that you may find in Christ and the Christian faith, as compared to the apathy and hostility of the Western 'post-Christian' world.

Conclusion

It is not possible in one brief chapter to go into more detail about what is involved in actively serving God's worldwide mission overseas; there are other people and places that can give you a fuller picture. Your local church leaders, world mission group and an appropriate world-mission agency can provide you with this, but you would be wise to 'shop around' the latter, particularly to ensure that they share the same gospel convictions as you do. There are many opportunities available for short-term mission opportunities overseas, which will help you work out if this kind of ministry is the right one for you.

What I hope to have left you with here are:

- an awareness of the need.
- a plea to think of what is best for the cause of God's global mission.
- the consideration of some of the costs involved, as well as the compensations.

If, with all this, you do become actively engaged in gospel ministry overseas then the fruit in the lives of others is in the Lord's hands but He will certainly use the experience to bring you to greater conformity 'to the likeness of his Son' (Romans 8 v 29) for His greater glory.

Cross-cultural ministry in the UK

Andrew Raynes

To be a cross-cultural minister in the UK—as anywhere else—requires a clear conviction about the gospel, namely that it is a message for all people everywhere. It is out of this conviction that that the motivation to cross cultures with the gospel flows.

The gospel is for all people everywhere

The implications of this truth reverberate through Luke's account of the growth of the Word of God in the Acts of the Apostles. So convinced is the apostle Paul of this truth that he can speak to the pagans in Athens of the God who 'now commands all people everywhere to repent' (Acts 17 v 30).

It's this conviction that will motivate and energise us to be in cross-cultural ministry, a ministry in which one interacts with people who have grown up learning values and lifestyle patterns that are different from one's own.

It's true, of course, that there is an element of cross-culture in all ministry—each of us has grown up within a particular culture that is distinct from others, even when those cultures may be superficially similar. Having moved from one end of England to the other a few years ago, I can testify that there is definitely a difference

'I have been looking for someone to tell me about Jesus...'

Al was converted in his second year at university, but it was some years later that he first thought of doing some kind of full-time Christian work.

'I realised that I should use my gifts—and I had a desire to teach and to reach out, so I did a year-long Bible-training course to test that leading. I did some teaching and preaching at the church placement I had, and, as a result of the encouragement of people there, I decided to pursue ministry long term.

'I realised that there were very few people doing mission work among the 100,000 Bangladeshis in the part of East London where I was based. There were lots of churches with social-action ministries, but very few concerned with preaching the gospel. Because of that need, my wife and I decided we should look at whether this was what we should make the focus of our ministry. So I spent a year shadowing an evangelist working on the Isle of Dogs.

'Now working part-time based at my church, I have adopted a two-pronged approach to outreach among the local Bangladeshis. The long-term approach is all about making friends, and building relationships with people and families and sharing the gospel with them over time.

'The second is plain, old-fashioned proclamation. We go out a few times a year and preach the gospel in the streets. Surprisingly, this has been very well received, as it is a culturally appropriate thing to do, and I often have great conversations with people afterwards. One of the first men I met through this work said to me: 'I have been looking for someone to tell me about Jesus for a long time.'

'We also do some tract distribution and letter-box drops in houses local to the church, and distribute Gospel portions in the local dialect for the area. My wife has opportunities to reach out to Bengali girls through a club on the local estate. This has given us some contacts with families there.

'The East End is a very stressful place to live—the physical environment is very oppressive. There is a lot of violence on the streets, and I've been mugged myself. But there is loads of encouraging stuff going on. It's easy to meet people. It's easy to talk about Christ. But it's very hard to go that step further: to make close friends with people, or to read the Bible one to one, or to get people on an evangelistic course.'

between Sussex and Lancashire cultures. What is appropriate in one culture is not necessarily appropriate in another.

But there are bigger challenges. Increasingly, the UK is becoming a place of racial diversity. According to the National Statistics Office, the minority ethnic population in Britain grew by 53% between 1991 and 2001, from 3.0 million in 1991 to 4.6 million in 2001, representing 7.9% of the total population. In Leicester, for example, over 25% of the population have an Indian ethnic origin.

Alongside those who are long-term residents, international students continue to come to the UK in significant numbers. In 2004, there were 300,000 international students in higher education (UKCOSA figures), many coming from countries such as China and Malaysia, where opportunities to hear the gospel are limited. Some estimates suggest that there may be a total of one million international students (including those in higher education and at language schools) in the UK.

Being flexible

People from cultures different from our own need to understand that the gospel is good news for everyone—whatever their religious or cultural background. And therefore we need to work hard at communicating the gospel, clothed in the culture of the people to whom we are ministering.

As the apostle Paul explains the character of his ministry to the Corinthian Christians, he speaks of his gospel-driven flexibility in 1 Corinthians 9. His ministry is shaped by a self-imposed slavery:

> I make myself a slave to everyone, to win as many as possible....
> I have become all things to all men so that by all possible means
> I might save some. **1 Corinthians 9 v 19-22**

Paul is totally inflexible about the content of the gospel—after all, it is 'the gospel of Christ' (v 12), and Paul is not at liberty to alter its content. At the same time though, how the apostle communicates the gospel is *very* negotiable. As Paul crosses cultures with the gospel, he was extremely flexible about the form his ministry took: 'To the Jews, I became like a Jew to win the Jews' (v 20). Hardly a big deal, you might think. After all, Paul was born a Jew. But that's not how Paul saw it. Christ, not his Jewish culture, was what now shaped his life. And because he wanted to see other Jews coming to Christ, he became like a Jew. He wanted to remove every possible barrier to the Jews hearing the gospel.

Similarly, among Gentiles, he 'became like one not having the law' (v 21). Paul's great passion was to 'win' people for Christ (v 19-21), or to 'save some' from the coming wrath of God (v 22b).

When speaking with Muslims or Jews in the UK, therefore, we need to take the trouble to understand their culture and religion—and then to be flexible in the ways that we share the gospel, without compromising the content of the message we proclaim.

This kind of flexibility does not come easily to any of us. And perhaps one of the best ways of growing into cross-cultural ministry in the UK is to leave it (at least temporarily!). It is a great help to step outside our own culture for a time, both to get a better understanding of our own culture, and also to be immersed in a different culture. Christian medical or language students who spend time abroad as part of their university courses often come back to the UK with new vision and skills for international student work.

Similarly, there are great opportunities to work in short-term overseas mission teams with IFES (International Fellowship of Evangelical Students), as well as other agencies such as Crosslinks and Interserve. It is perhaps no surprise to find that many of the people currently involved in cross-cultural ministry in the UK have themselves spent time in ministry overseas. They have had to deal with the issues of crossing cultures at first hand—and have learned to recognise the difference between culture and the gospel.

The shape of cross-cultural ministry

The opportunities for cross-cultural ministry in the UK vary considerably. Among international students, some churches and individuals are active in providing hospitality, offering friendship by inviting international students into their homes for a meal or for a weekend. Some Christian Unions work together with local churches to run a café where international students can meet and be helped to adjust to the UK.

One church in a busy university town runs a weekly 'Globe Café' with a programme of events ranging from a *Blue Peter* evening to an introduction to the British Royal Family. The same church runs a weekly Bible study for people whose first language is not English, focusing on one of the gospels. Other churches use the *English Made Easy* version of the *Christianity Explored* course, which is especially geared to the needs of internationals. *Friends International* has staff workers around the country ministering to international students, and also runs training events to equip people for cross-cultural ministry. Their ministry is explained at www.friendsinternational.org.uk.

Elsewhere, cross-cultural ministry focuses less on students and more on those who are long-term UK residents. There are some cultural groups where there is already a vibrant Christian community, especially among African communities in London. But among others—Asian-heritage Muslims in Bradford, or Hindus in Leicester, for example—there is a massive need for gospel-hearted churches and individuals to do the hard work of building bridges into what are often fairly segregated communities—and to cross those bridges with the gospel in culturally appropriate ways.

Our church in Lancashire was fairly abruptly launched into cross-cultural ministry by the arrival of a large number of asylum seekers in our area some years ago. Because few of them had a good understanding of English, we started a weekly international

---

Starting from scratch

Rosanne works in Oxford with UCCF, but has a long-term interest in reaching out to internationals, particularly those from Japan. 'Oxford is packed with international students, and in addition to the universities there are masses of language-school, and summer-school students who come each year, often with their wives. There are also a lot of Japanese women here in their late 20s who have worked a while at home, got disillusioned with life, and come to the UK for a year to find a new life, and learn the language.

'Family expectations are enormous for many Asians: there is huge pressure on them to be part of the traditional way of living and doing things. For many of them, therefore, being away from home gives them the freedom to investigate something new and different. At the church I am part of, we run an evening meal and a Bible study for international students. They mostly come through the invitation of a Christian friend, but stay because of the strong friendships they form. We also run a small social programme of outings and other events to try and build relationships with each other.'

Rosanne previously worked in Japan with students, so she has a better point of contact than most: 'I've got the language, and because I have lived there and travelled around a lot, I can talk about TV programmes and can often make a connection with where they are from.

'Because there is so little known about Christianity in Japan, we are often starting from scratch, with really basic things: that there is one creator God, and that Jesus was a real historical person—not some kind of mythical western super-hero. And they don't know what it is to live as a Christian, so it is especially important to share your life with them.'

evening where they could meet for food—and also read the Bible together.

We found a group of Iranians who were especially responsive to the gospel and who began to come regularly to our Sunday services. In order to accommodate their need to hear the gospel in a culturally appropriate way, we made a point of having the Bible read in both English and Farsi at our evening service. We also began an enquirers group for Iranians, using a series of videos in Farsi. Becoming 'like an Iranian' meant learning to appreciate the food they cooked and trying to learn some of their language. When they were being faced with suspicion and outright hostility from many local people, these small gestures went a long way in helping break down some of the cultural barriers between us and build genuine friendships.

Among the Asian-heritage population, we have struggled to make inroads for the gospel—although, ironically, it is far easier to speak about the Lord Jesus with an Asian Muslim than with many of the white English that we come across. A few church members are involved in regular home visiting—and some of these visits have matured into opportunities for evangelistic Bible study. At the local primary school, which is predominantly Asian, we have recently started a weekly lunchtime Bible club for older children.

In other parts of the UK, churches have come together to support a specialised ministry to Asians within their town or city. In one northern city, two people are engaged in full-time ministry to Asians (alongside a team of volunteers)—visiting homes, running small low-key Bible studies with families or individuals and operating a bookstall on the local market as well as providing help and nurture for local Asian Christians.

A ministry for all believers

We need to be careful that we do not think of cross-cultural ministry as necessarily a specialist ministry for the few. While there will be some whose ministry will be given to a particular people-group or culture, all Christians are called upon to behave and speak for the glory of God in whatever cultural context they find themselves.

The apostle Paul commends his own ministry as a pattern for the whole church to follow in their relationships with people of different cultures (1 Corinthians 10 v 31 – 11 v 1). This is a pattern that involves 'seeking... the good of many, so that they may be saved' (verse 33). Through such faithful and flexible living and speaking it will be seen that the gospel transcends culture, and that it really is for all people everywhere.

Women's ministry

Carrie Sandom

> I commend to you our sister Phoebe, a servant of the church in Cenchrea. I ask you to receive her in the Lord in a way worthy of the saints and to give her any help she may need from you, for she has been a great help to many people, including me.
>
> **Romans 16 v 1**

SO STARTS THE FINAL CHAPTER of Paul's letter to the Romans, where he commends the ministries of numerous gospel partners. What is perhaps most interesting to note is just how many of them are women. Paul often has a very bad press today but, contrary to popular opinion, he was not a misogynist. Instead he was a great proponent of women's ministry, provided it was modelled by godly women who understood and upheld the biblical parameters placed upon them.

Equal but different

The Bible teaches that both men and women are made in the image of God and, as a result, are equal before Him in status, dignity and humanity (Genesis 1 v 27). They are also equal inheritors of the promises God made to Abraham (Galatians 3 v 26-29), because there is now no distinction between Jews or Greeks, slaves or free, male or female. There is also no distinction between men and women on how spiritual gifts are distributed (1 Corinthians 12 v 7) although, when it comes to teaching gifts, there are differences in how these gifts are to be used.

Jesus' own attitude to women was revolutionary for His day and clearly upheld the equality of men and women. He spoke to women in public; He valued their companionship and their service; He taught them both individually and alongside men, and commended Mary for making His teaching a priority when other responsibilities might have distracted her from listening to Him (Luke 10 v 42). The gospels record that women were the first eye-witnesses to the resurrection and were given the task of telling others what they had seen (Matthew 28 v 7, Mark 16 v 7 and John 20 v 17), even though a woman's testimony was not thought to be reliable in the law courts at the time.

There is no doubt that Jesus highly valued the ministry of women and, like Paul, commended them for their service of the gospel. But we need also to remember that Jesus did not appoint women as His apostles—a unique foundational role reserved for a select group of men (Acts 1 v 21-26), and Paul never appointed women to be overseers of the local church (1 Timothy 3 v 1-7, Titus 1 v 5-9). Women have a unique contribution to make to the life of the local church, but it is not the same as the role of men.

Modelled by the Trinity

But why, when so much of His treatment of women was revolutionary for His day, did Jesus not introduce identical roles for men and women in the local church? In our day and age it seems almost incredible that equality of status doesn't also mean equality of function.

The answer to this question lies at the very heart of the Godhead itself. In the Trinity we see a pattern of relationships that shows us how it is possible for equality of being to co-exist with diversity of function. God the Father, Son and Holy Spirit are equally divine, but each has a different function within the Godhead. Moreover, there is a definite ordering of their relationships—so the Son submits Himself to His Father's will (Mark 14 v 36, John 6 v 38), and the Holy Spirit submits both to the Father's will and the Son's will (John 14 v 16-17, John 14 v 26 and John 16 v 13-15).

The pattern for family life and church family life

It is this pattern of relationships that is to be modelled in family life and in church family life, as God orders His creation to reflect the pattern of relationships within the Godhead itself (1 Corinthians 11 v 3). Because of the order and purpose of their creation, wives are to submit to their husbands in everything, in recognition of the fact that husbands are head of the family as Christ is head of the church (Ephesians 5 v 22-24). Similarly, husbands are to love their wives just as Christ loved the church and gave Himself up for her. This is the way God has ordered their relationships with each other and Christian marriage cannot function well without it. Yet this does not mean they are not equal – each of them needs the other to play their part, if their marriage is to reflect the way the Lord Jesus Christ relates to His bride, the church (Ephesians 5 v 25-33).

When it comes to roles within the church family, the same pattern of relationships applies. Because of the order and purpose of their creation, men are to have leadership responsibilities that women do not share. It is not appropriate for a woman to teach or have authority over men (1 Timothy 2 v 11-13), although it is entirely appropriate for a woman to teach and train other women (Titus 2 v 3-5). In fact, there is a role here that is uniquely theirs, because, while men *can* teach the Bible to women, they cannot model to them what godly womanhood looks like in practice.

The areas mentioned in this Titus passage that need to be modelled effectively constitute three different spheres of life—the first involves relationships within the family, the second involves purity and self-control, and the third involves the whole area of work. Men are needed to model to other men what it means to be godly in these areas, but only women can model to women what it means to be godly women. The complementarity of men and women in ministry is therefore as important as it is for husbands and wives in marriage, as each needs the other to do their part. Only then will the people of God be properly pastored by the Word of God.

Other passages to consider

- **1 Corinthians 11 v 2-16**: While men and women can pray and prophesy in public it seems that the way in which they do so needs to reflect their gender differences and model male headship. Some would argue that women can therefore preach/prophesy from time to time, although not all evangelicals are convinced that this is compatible with the prohibition in 1 Timothy 2.

- **1 Corinthians 14 v 26-35**: This cannot be a blanket prohibition on women speaking or Paul is contradicting what he has said in chapter 11. He is concerned that good order should be established and maintained in the church. To that end, it is not appropriate for women to interrupt proceedings. Instead they should remain silent and direct any questions they have to their husbands at home. In this way, the important role a husband has in teaching and discipling his wife is demonstrated and upheld.

- **1 Timothy 2 v 14**: Paul has just warned Timothy to avoid the false teaching of two men (1 Timothy 1 v 19-20), so this cannot mean that women are always going to lead the church into error – if that were so, why would Paul encourage them to teach women? Verse 14 seems to follow straight on from the reasoning of v 13 and serves as an example of the disorder that ensues when God's order and rule is disobeyed.

- **1 Timothy 2 v 15**: Paul affirms the bearing and nurture of children as a God-given role that is uniquely for women. Eve was deceived when she ate the forbidden fruit and took the lead over her husband, causing him to sin as well. Women will be kept safe from Satan's deception, if they accept God's ordering of relationships within the family and the church family. Paul is not saying that all women will have children of their own, anymore than he's saying that all men will be church leaders, but each has a role that is uniquely reserved for them.

The range of opportunities on offer

A growing number of evangelical churches are recognising the need to employ women on their staff teams. A range of different ministries is open to them—children's ministry, youth ministry, student ministry and ministry to women of all ages and stages of life. What each of these ministries involves varies from church to church, but most will be involved in teaching the Bible to small groups, either in a talk or seminar format, as well as in group and one-to-one Bible studies. Some will be involved in speaking to larger groups, sometimes evangelistically, and some may preach from time to time if the individual church thinks it is appropriate for women to do so.

Opportunities for women in para-church organisations like UCCF, Scripture Union and the Titus Trust are also on the increase. The work they are involved in is often more specialised and, as a result, potentially quite isolating. Even if the women are working as part of a team, the day-to-day responsibilities of visiting schools or Christians Unions is mostly done alone. This can mean that it is harder to demonstrate the principle of male headship, especially when people see both men and women doing exactly the same work—but never together.

This is also true for women working overseas, where the need to increase labourers for the harvest field is arguably even greater. Many of today's missionary organisations would not have survived into the 21st century were it not for the courage of scores of single women who were prepared to take the gospel to new situations on their own. But in an ideal world it would be a team of both men and women doing this pioneering work together.

Some practical considerations

Training

The main denominations only rarely provide the funding to train women who do not wish to be overall leaders in churches. This means that those who share the convictions of this chapter about women's ministry are likely to have to fund themselves if they wish to attend theological college. For many, this is prohibitively expensive, although grants can be obtained from a growing number of trusts that are keen to see women gain access to the best training possible.

One factor related to the issue of how women are to be trained is the number of years they anticipate being in 'paid' ministry. This is something that men don't usually have to consider, because the 'career' structure for them is much more obvious, and the changes brought about by marriage and parenthood don't usually affect their work to the same degree. But for women it is very different, as marriage and motherhood rightly change their priorities dramatically. While wives and mothers certainly don't stop being involved in gospel ministry, they are generally involved in different ways compared to single women. It is not unreasonable therefore to consider the 'return' one might expect from a woman who undergoes three years residential training, in order to assess whether it is a wise investment of time and financial resources.

The Cornhill Training Course in London is one accessible and easily affordable option for both men and women. It is essentially a Bible-handling course and encourages students to learn how to teach the different types of Biblical genre with faithfulness and clarity. The women's ministry stream is an integral part of the year-long course and has been developed to encourage women to think through what Word ministry looks like for them as women. It seeks to promote a complementarian model of ministry, while

'A lot more than coffee and chat...'

Andrea was teaching in a junior school in Croydon, and ran a couple of Bible clubs. 'I wanted to be better equipped to do that, so I enroled at a Bible College part time for a couple of years, fully intending to go back into full-time Christian schools work.

'During my time at College, I did a couple of missions—one in Blackburn, and one overseas in the Gambia. At these, I had an opportunity to do talks and Bible studies with women. Up to that time, I had a bit of a stereotype of what women's workers were actually like: rather old fashioned, a bit 'twin set and pearl', and rather too serious (although the women's worker at my church was nothing like that!). But over that time, God really excited me with the idea of working with women. I hadn't thought about it before, and wasn't really up for it—but I began to see the need, the potential and the opportunities. In the past I had resisted going on our church women's weekend away; I thought: 'it's weird and unnatural to have an all-women thing like that.' But when I went, I found that it was people just like me—ordinary women—and we had a terrific time, learning, praying, growing and having lots of fun together.'

Andrea is now the Associate for Womens' Ministry at St Nicholas Church in Sevenoaks. 'I am the first women's worker at this church. There was already a lot going on for women, but my job has been to pull it all together, make the links between the groups and develop the work. Although I do a fair bit of admin, my key role is teaching the Bible to women, and helping other women to do that; it's a lot more than just 'coffee and chat.' I'm involved with various day-time groups: Bible studies, mums and toddlers, and a *Christianity Explored* group. There are huge opportunities with young mums, and I spend a lot of time encouraging Christian women to build relationships with non-Christians and reach out to them.

'At times, I feel overwhelmed by the size of the job and the needs that are there. But that's a good thing, because it makes me rely on God for the outcome of what I am able to do. It's really important in this work to get the proper support. I'm part of a really great, encouraging ministry team, which meets regularly to pray and plan. I also get terrific support from a network of women in ministry, and have kept up contacts with lots of people from my time in Cornhill.'

appreciating that how it works in practice may vary in different contexts. The course explores the different theological positions held by evangelicals on the role of women in the church, and encourages the students to find ways of working within them, without compromising their consciences. It also considers issues that are pertinent to women—eg: ministry expectations, length of time in 'paid' ministry, funding, deployment and opportunities for further training.

In recent years the emergence of various part-time ministry training courses around the country has opened up new possibilities for training 'on-the-job'. They provide Bible exposition, doc-

Annie's song

Annie trained as a nurse, and worked in the NHS for many years. 'I'd gone as far as I wanted to in nursing, and when I had the chance to take a year out, I joined the first year of Cornhill, and subsequently joined UCCF as a staff worker.

'After six years with UCCF, I went back to nursing for a while before I was offered a job at City Evangelical Church in Birmingham as the women's pastoral worker.

'When I first arrived, there were only 40 or so people in the church, mainly students, but there were also a few elderly folk to look after as well. I love seeing people grow up in Jesus, and now that the church has grown the work is quite varied and challenging. I don't have the structure of lots of groups and meetings that many women's workers have—I do loads of one-to-ones. This pattern of work can be quite exhausting, and the downside is that it can also be quite lonely, although the staff teams' subsequent move into offices has helped with this.

'It's a privilege to be able to do this work as a single woman— it's a lifestyle that would be difficult for a married woman to maintain. It feels a bit like being a mum to the younger students, or a sister to my contemporaries, and being a daughter to the older ones. I'm always looking for natural opportunities to encourage them in Christ.'

trine and pastoral theology along with practical teaching workshops to help people hone their teaching skills. Most people work in local-church placements the rest of the week, and meet regularly with a supervisor for prayer and further theological reflection.

Challenges

There are various challenges to be faced in ministry. The most common challenge for women in ministry is how to work out their role as a woman and model male headship appropriately. This is not particularly surprising when many are pioneering roles in contexts where women have never worked before.

Women often cite emotional exhaustion as another big challenge. Men and women work very differently and relate to their own sex very differently. Many observe that women tend to get more emotionally involved with people than men do, and will take longer to switch off at the end of the day. One way of illustrating this is to compare the way men and women conduct one-to-one ministry—pastoral interviews, Bible studies, etc. Men will often be able to see three people one after the other with no break in between and take just 45 minutes seeing each one. Woman can rarely see more than two people in a row without a decent break, and will take a minimum of an hour and a half seeing each one.

It is therefore unrealistic to assume that women can achieve the same as men in terms of the quantity of work done or people seen. We may be putting ourselves under unnecessary pressure by assuming that men and women do things in the same way—but they don't. Allan and Barbara Pease's book *Why men don't listen and women can't read maps* (Orion, 1999) is not a Christian book, but the observations they make about how men and women work differently, and the unrealistic expectations they often have of each other, are quite illuminating.

Deployment

Women who are looking for full-time 'paid' ministry opportunities need to have realistic expectations about the future. The number of churches that have employed women in a full-time 'paid' capacity right through to retirement can be counted on the fingers of one hand. While the number of churches employing women is on

---

'I love the variety…'

Sue has been a full-time worker for 33 years, and has worked in a huge variety of roles during her ministry. Her first job was as a parish worker in an Anglican church in Dagenham, and she then moved to Bristol to work with students and people in their 20s and 30s. After a job combining youthwork and homegroup co-ordination in Streatham, Sue joined the staff of All Nations Christian College as Admissions Tutor, assessing applicants, and helping with the pastoral care of students. More student work in Norwich was followed by four years running Rushmore holidays—a series of camps for girls. Sue has now returned to at a church in Bristol, as a pastoral co-ordinator mainly working with women; here she also gets to lead services and speak at all-age services. Sue also chairs the personnel advisory group of a mission agency, interviewing and assessing candidates.

'What I love about this work is the sheer variety. I love working with all ages; I love meeting people at all stages of life—and I love sharing the gospel with people. I find that women are willing to open up and chat about personal issues, including spiritual things. And there are so many opportunities, as, on the whole, women have more time.

'I've often struggled with being the only woman on an all-male team; and working out how to develop a complementary role can be quite difficult. The job could easily take every waking moment—it can become all consuming. It may be because I am single, but I need to work hard at keeping up with friends, and a maintaining social life outside of church life.

'When I went into parish work 30 years ago there were loads of jobs available, but, since women's ordination, there have been far fewer positions available for unordained women. It's been encouraging that more Bible-teaching churches have been taking people on in recent years. It's an area of ministry that is rich with possibilities, but is often under-resourced.'

---

the increase, most are likely to employ a 25-year old for 2-3 years, rather than a 40-year old for 20 years. Many women do leave 'paid' ministry when they marry and have children—perhaps returning, albeit in an unpaid capacity, after the children have left home.

Those who don't marry need to have something else to fall back on, and should not expect to find full-time 'paid' employment right through to retirement. I therefore think it wise for women to have some sort of secular work experience/training before they enter 'paid' ministry. This means that local churches need to be careful not to encourage them into full-time 'paid' ministry too soon.

Conclusion

Following pressure from equal-rights lobbyists, several UK denominations have ruled that women can lead local church congregations on their own. Sadly, the growing liberalism of many of these denominations has set a course for continuing doctrinal drift. The denominations may not be in very good shape, but God is still sovereign and His Word will never pass away—whatever the number of unbiblical motions passed by denominational synods and councils.

However, what the enemy intends for harm, God often intends for good. One very positive consequence of this growing liberalism is the galvanization of conservative evangelicals to ensure that the biblical pattern for women's ministry is affirmed and maintained. The number of churches who are employing women (albeit outside the formal structures of most denominations) is very encouraging. There should also be a snowball effect in all this—as more women are engaged in appropriate gospel ministries and able to teach women about them, other women will be encouraged to follow in their footsteps.

One ordained woman who refused to take charge of a local church on headship grounds, and works instead as an assistant minister in Basingstoke, told me about her annual ministerial review. She met with the denominational advisor for women clergy for over an hour, and talked with her about the work she was involved in and her plans for the future. At the end of the interview, the adviser said it was the first time she had come across someone who didn't want to move up the career ladder, and was fascinated to hear how contented she seemed to be. She remarked: 'I think you are the first ordained woman I have ever met who is neither angry, frustrated nor depressed.'

We shouldn't be surprised at this. Those who take God's Word seriously and seek to live it out will prove that what He says in His Word is true and for their good. A growing number of women are committing themselves to the biblical pattern for women's ministry and are content to live within the parameters God sets them in His Word. We must pray that God will continue to raise up gospel workers, both men and women, and send them into His harvest field.

Youth and children's ministry

Roger Fawcett

Ryan and his sister are shopping in the local town centre. They meet a Mormon with a clip board and get talking to him. They tell him where they live and invite him round. The Mormon visits, more than once, and the three of them talk about where Mormonism and Christianity differ, and the truth of the gospel. Several times Ryan calls his youth leader late at night to ask for advice and prayer.

Chris struggles with one person in the Christian union at school. There is a Christadelphian girl in it who believes very different things to him. But whenever he thinks he should confront her, he can't think of what to say. Together with a friend and his youth leader, he is able to meet and pray and study the Bible to equip himself to face this challenge.

Jackie is new at school. She has determined to stand up for her faith despite the dangers of teasing and bullying. She tells the cool girls that a boy has to be a Christian for her to be interested, not just attractive. She makes it clear in class what she thinks about bawdy jokes and sexual innuendos. She challenges her teacher with her real faith that is not just a 'Sundays only' faith like the teacher's own.

OUR CHILDREN AND YOUNG PEOPLE are on the front line of the battle with this crooked and depraved generation. This might sound like hyperbole or scare tactics, but it is true. The pressure in the playground to conform is immense, as the real-life examples above show. What should we do on Sunday morning or evening with our Christian young people and children? Should we tell them to be of good cheer because they shine like stars? Or should we equip them with the one thing that will make a difference in their generation—the gospel, God's word of life.

> Do everything without complaining or arguing, so that you may become blameless and pure, children of God without fault in a crooked and depraved generation, in which you shine like stars in the universe as you hold out the word of life. **Phil 2 v 14-16**

When people refer to these verses, they often get as far as 'shining like stars' and then stop. It is nice to think of ourselves, Christian believers, as the only light in a bleak world; the moral bedrock, the upright and dependable ones in a world that is quickly going down the drain. We need to finish reading Paul's thought and ignore the verse division. What makes these Philippians shine like stars is the fact that they hold out the Word of life. If they go on holding out that word of life, says Paul, his labour is not in vain. And even if he dies, he will be glad and the Philippians should rejoice with him. That is our challenge too, to hold out the word of life in a crooked and depraved generation.

It is a sad fact of the evangelical Christian world that there are not enough good people around teaching the Bible to both children and young people. There are two prevailing attitudes that contribute to this in some measure. Both attitudes are misguided and present a danger to Bible-centred youth work.

First, there is the attitude that working with young people is a very important and worthy thing to be doing, but that the Bible really gets in the way, and inhibits the growth of youth and children's work. Many churches, even large evangelical ones, have a youth and children's track that may *use* the Bible, but does not put an emphasis on high-quality Bible teaching. The Bible is there because we are Christians, but the real deal in youth work is worship or mentoring; the real deal in children's work is play or entertainment.

Secondly, there is the attitude that the Bible should be at the centre of what we do, and it should be correctly handled and taught very well, but youth and children's work is really something we do to explore our calling to ministry or as a stepping stone. After all, working with adults or students is the really vibrant and important ministry, and becoming a pastor or vicar is the sign that you are really serious. Many churches, even large evangelical ones, still consider someone whose love is teaching the Bible to young people a bit of a poor country cousin, not involved in real ministry.

Both these attitudes need stamping out in our churches. The current leaders, both lay and ordained, need to change the way they view youth and children's ministry. Training organisations need to recognise the legitimacy of full-time, long-term youth and children's workers. And those people considering Christian ministry need to give serious thought to whether they are called to this ministry, not just as a half-way house, but as something worth giving ten or twenty years, or even a whole career to.

What are the needs?

First and foremost, the need is for the Bible to be taught well. It is an old cliché that today's young people are tomorrow's church leaders. And while it is certainly a cliché there is truth to it. One of the reasons for the proliferation of liberalism today is the growth in liberal scholarship during the 20th century. The church leaders today grew up during that period of growth. What climate are our own young people growing up in? What effect will it have on their future stability as Christians?

David's story

David Whitehouse worked as a youth minister for many years at St Peter's, Harold Wood. He now ministers to children and young people in Manchester.

Why are you still working with young people after 14 years?

I started because I had a love for the age group and a passion to see them won for Christ. Now, although I'm slightly longer of tooth and shorter of hair than I used to be, I still have the same love and passion. I am also convinced that young people and children need Christian maturity in those who pastorally care for them, rather than simply leaders who are "young enough to relate to the kids".

Why did you decide to keep doing it after ordination?

The pastoral oversight of youth ministry carries with it the same responsibilities as any of the other ordained staff. So ordination for me was never about a move away from youth ministry, but a way of identifying the nature of that ministry. Why should youth ministry be considered as simply a training ground for 'proper ministry', rather than a responsibility to teach the Word of God and care for people at the most impressionable and rapidly changing stage of life?

Ordination is not a road that everyone going into youth ministry will want to follow, but it has helped me to go through the same rigorous process of testing and training that any other pastor-teacher would need to submit themselves to. I also hoped it would help others to treat youth ministry as a genuine long-term calling.

What are your priorities as a youth minister?

My first priority is to support Christian parents in the spiritual upbringing of children, to provide them with the tools and resources to bring up their children 'in the training and instruction of the Lord'. For too long, youth ministry has colluded with the idea that the best thing a parent can do is to send their child along to the youth group, then stand well back. Without stifling the ability of young people to work out their own identity, I want to ensure that the Christian family is the primary context for a young person's spiritual growth.

The more pressing reason for good Bible teaching is the welfare of the young people themselves. Our children need good teaching so that they are grounded in the Scriptures from childhood. (We also need to teach parents how to teach—another story). Our adolescents need teaching so that Christianity becomes more than a crutch for the weak, or entertainment for an hour on Friday night.

They need to be taught the truth of our faith. Teenagers need to be taught because otherwise they will not put down an anchor, and may drift away once they leave the sheltered atmosphere of the youth group.

There is undoubtedly also a need for evangelism among young people today. We are no longer a society where people grow up with even a rudimentary knowledge of Bible stories and Christian ethics. Ministry among young people and children needs people who are dedicated to, and capable of, getting the whole gospel out generation by generation.

The need is for people who are able communicators, believing in the truths of the Bible and the power of the Holy Spirit to change lives. Those in youth ministry need to be able to encourage young people as they share their faith.

The need for a recognition of youth and children's work as a *bona fide* ministry has already been mentioned. For someone considering this ministry it is an important consideration. Is youth-work more than just a stepping stone? Are the jobs that are available taking the youth or children's worker seriously in the package that is provided? Is the proper time given to a youth ministry post? In other words, is there a recognition that work with both children or young people needs to be more than just a couple of years—it takes that long just to learn the names!

The Trials of Trevor

Trevor Pearce grew up in Chessington, SW London, and became the youth worker at the church he was converted in. He now works at the Bridge Chapel in Liverpool, where he leads a large team of volunteers.

What is your daily routine like as a youth worker?
It is so important to plan out your week , otherwise you will lose it. If you are not self-disciplined in youth work—if you can't control your diary or your time—then you will be ineffective. I split my day into three, and then try to only work two of them (it often doesn't work!). I aim to keep the mornings free for my own study. One-to-ones I like to do at either breakfast, or after lunch. Apart from my evening clubs and regular meetings, I also do two school lunchtime CU meetings each week. I spend a lot of time investing in the leaders I work with in the various groups the church runs. I spend time sharing the vision for Bible-centred youth work and help them with their talks.

What are the particular difficulties that people new to youth work face?
Loneliness! There is a terrible lack of support for most youth workers. Ministers don't really understand that most youth workers are new to Christian ministry, and very young. They dump the youth work on them, and too often haven't set aside the time to give them a proper structure and encouragement to keep going. They either work themselves ragged, or else are lazy and waste their time.

Youth workers often have to manage bigger teams than the minister does. Most churches run their youth and children's work on an army of volunteers. Young men and women are placed in the situation where they have to lead people who may have been doing their job for decades, and often wrongly! This is very hard—how do you train, lead or even rebuke an older person? This is where they need the proper support of the senior pastor—and too often fail to get it.

Dealing with parents is another area where they too often do not get the support they need. Parents will be very vocal if their kid comes home not having enjoyed the youth group, and often place unfair pressure on youth leaders to 'tone down' the Bible-teaching element of the group. This is where a youth leader needs the support and confidence of, and firm backing from, the top.

What are the rewards of this ministry?

Many churches recognise the need for youth and children's workers. Many churches act on this need and employ one, two or many more. Youth and children's work is a vacuum that will fill up and go on needing leaders. Unfortunately, the vacuum is not necessarily filled with good people. But the quick-fix option brings instant results: the youth group swells, the Sunday school is fun and the holiday clubs are epic. Despite this outcome, some questions remain. Where are all those young people when they hit their twenties? Do they still attend church even though it is boring? Are they still disciplined enough to read their Bibles and pray regularly even though it's a slog?

Don't misunderstand, there is plenty of room for fun and laughter in youth work. The youth leader's job is not to be a kill-joy. But there can be so much more. This really is the best job in world. Seeing young people commit their lives to the Lord, get switched on to His Word, get stuck into church and evangelise their friends is a huge reward.

But the best rewards in youth work come over a longer timescale, and these are the rewards worth aiming for. The youth-group member who goes off to college with a real desire to live a godly life and continue with their faith. The dawning realisation that the last few years of week-by-week struggle at the coal face of a Bible-teaching group has paid off. Something has gone in, the children have understood an important truth about God, and have a desire to follow Jesus.

There is a world of difference between being able to fill a hall with young people and actually feeding them properly on God's Word. As Paul wrote in Philippians, we hold out the Word of life to them. That is how we get the young people across the finishing line. Paul wrote elsewhere (Colossians 1 v 28) that his aim was to 'present everyone perfect in Christ'. And that is the aim of Bible-centred youth ministry—to present young people perfect in Christ on the day of the Lord's return.

Building the urban church downtown

Ken Moulder

FOR THE LAST 17 YEARS I have been vicar of St. Oswald's Church, Walkergate, which is situated in the east of Newcastle upon Tyne. The parish is designated an urban-priority area, which means there is a high level of unemployment and many single-parent families. The population is predominantly white working class and there is a high percentage of council housing, although one part of the parish is more 'up market' (I suppose one would say lower middle class), where the folk are owner occupiers. I am only the second vicar of St. Oswald's, my predecessor having been in the post for 37 years.

I do not have a 'one size fits all' solution to the problem of gospelling people in the urban sprawl. Therefore, some of what I say may not be appropriate for the situation in which you may be working, or thinking about working in. It seems to me that much of what I have to say applies in any and every situation, and is not unique to ministry in a non-book, working-class culture.

Prior to my arrival at St. Oswald's, there had been no gospel ministry. The services were decidedly sacramental with celebrations of Holy Communion each Sunday and midweek.

The congregation numbered around 40 ageing folk and a handful of children, who were taught in one Sunday School group for 0-11s. There were no teenagers or young people.

The church had no clearly defined theology and was, in my view, one generation from extinction. This was easily illustrated from church life. Most of the men (about a dozen or so) were Freemasons, as was the previous vicar. Being invited to the Masons, I discovered, was a sign of upward mobility in the working-class culture of the area. The church shared annually in a joint service with the local Unitarians (who, among other things, deny the divinity of the Lord Jesus), and the church was financed by a weekly cash-prize lottery. There was a big gambling culture with tickets sold in thousands around the area.

So, on arrival, there were a few things to work out in the 'church', never mind gospelling the area of Walkergate. However the situation did, and still does, represent a terrific missionary opportunity. The Bible teaches that the gospel bears fruit wherever planted (Colossians 1 v 6), so, together with my family, we decided to go to work there. We had seen gospel fruitfulness at Harold Wood in a large middle-class church—a very privileged position in which to train—and had enjoyed a taste of working in an urban working-class situation, teaching the gospel in Barnsley as curate in charge of a daughter church. Here was a mission field to work out gospel principles from ground level!

Two convictions

Two convictions underpinned our work in Walkergate.

First, it is our conviction that the 'gospel' is the power of God for salvation. Paul states this quite clearly in Romans 1 v 16-17. Power for ministry among the working class, non-book culture is to be found in exactly the same place as it is for work among the pin-striped suits of the City of London. We are committed to the message of the gospel—of Jesus' life, death and resurrection—as the means by which God, by His Spirit, brings people from spiritual darkness to light. This is the message that needs to be heard. All types of people need to hear the message of the gospel, whether they are people who have good paper qualifications and enjoyed years of formal education, or people who left school at the first opportunity and seldom open a book.

The second conviction which underpins our work is the belief that the Bible is sufficient for the life of faith. 2 Timothy 3 v 16-17 is very clear on this. In the Bible, God has given to us all that is needed to bring people to spiritual life, and to enable them to grow to maturity in Christ, so I do not need to go anywhere else for special help, strength and direction for the work of the gospel ministry and godly living. So, if I want people to become Christians and grow in maturity of faith, I must bring them under the teaching of the Word of God.

Our priority, therefore, is to present the message of the Bible by all means. This is not only achieved by preaching to the gathered congregation, but also through small group and individual work. We seek to encourage friendship evangelism in order to bring folk under the sound of the gospel.

In more recent years the Church Council of St. Oswald's has come up with a mission statement[1] to reflect these convictions. It's a statement to which we refer regularly in our planning, and which enables us to evaluate our work year on year, to see that we are letting God's purpose set the agenda for the way we spend our energy and time. There were many scuffles with the congregation to get the gospel on the agenda, but now everything we do in Walkergate flows from these two convictions.

---

1. Mission Statement: 'To know Christ and to make Him known by proclaiming and living out the biblical gospel. To teach and explain the Bible in order that people may come to repentance and faith and grow to maturity in Christ.'

Applying the convictions

In one way we were fortunate as there was very, very little on the regular programme at St. Oswald's when I arrived with the family. Therefore, there was plenty of space to introduce new things without needing to take away all the old junk at one go, although the lottery and the joint service with the Unitarians had to go pretty much straight away.

My primary aims were to teach the Bible at every opportunity and to reach the unchurched. To reinforce this, I was encouraging Christians to be making use of their friendships to bring others under the teaching of the gospel

From the beginning, I have worked from the principle that preaching is possible. God uses a message to bring us salvation so it follows that it needs to be taught and explained. The fact that people have few paper qualifications does not mean that they are incapable of listening to reasoned explanation, of following an argument or understanding what the Scriptures are saying. It is mistaken and insulting to think this way. Worse, it suggests God provided inadequately for certain types of people by giving us a word! So, we provided Bibles and preached. The congregation at St. Oswald's was not used to preaching, so I started small, with 12-15 minutes, and slowly built up to the present 20-25 minutes. I preach at every meeting, including mid-week communion, to emphasise the centrality of God's Word.

I have come to appreciate that small-group learning is crucial, with the make-up of the groups spanning anything from a couple in their own home, to four to six people meeting at a convenient venue. In the Walkergate situation, I began with one Bible-study group for all-comers. In order to make these groups as user-friendly and unthreatening as possible, we did not sing or share thoughts; we simply read the Bible and sought to understand and apply it. Before long we required an evangelistic Bible-study group. We devised our own package called *Taking a Look Group* which went through *Two Ways to Live* in four weeks.

Church services

I inherited a service pattern of 9.30am Holy Communion and, at 6.30pm, 1662 Evening Prayer. These I maintained, initially, but added a more accessible Sunday meeting for families at 11.00am, following a friendly, easy-to-use format, that used a single card, rather than a whole service book. This was something outsiders could come to, follow and not be lost. The meeting was very small for the first two years—less than dozen, so newcomers were conspicuous—but there has been steady and encouraging growth over the years to our present position of around a hundred regulars.

The Toddler Group, which we started up for parents and pre-school children, was a key way to show our commitment to the area. The high-quality provision of the group, both then and now, made it very popular in the area and, unlike other groups, had the added attraction of being free. It has, over the years, proved a fertile ground for the Christians who manage the group to speak about Christ, and invite friends made there along to special events.

After around three years, our people resources grew. By then we had an assistant minister, so we could respond to the growing number of opportunities. We began to appoint lay assistants (for a year) to support the work. We enjoyed good financial support from other gospel congregations in Newcastle and around the country. All the time we are seeking to build cumulative or overlapping contact with families in the area, which we consider key to the work in Walkergate.

Initiatives

Some examples of later developments in the work are:

- **The open youth club work**: which happens on two nights each week. The children who come along are rough and ready and the demands on leaders are high. We don't have an epilogue at this, but occasionally run a *Taking a Look* group. It has been the means of encouraging several youngsters to go on Christian venture holidays. Through this work there has been a steady trickle of youngsters connected with the church family, and there is a midweek bible-study group for teenagers.

- **The children's summer holiday club**: a week of Bible teaching and activities for about 90 children. It is very popular and demand always exceeds availability of places. Activities for families at the end of the week—a barbecue on the Saturday and a special on the Sunday—have provided valuable contacts and, like the youth clubs, it has been a means of developing very good PR in the area.

Leadership development was, and still is, high on our agenda. With the church council there was much to correct in the early days, and it continues to be a case of explain, explain, explain.

With the growth of Bible-study groups more leaders are needed; these leaders are prepared for the task through weekly preparation sessions. A growing number of people are signing up for the *Moore College* course, although few take the exams.

A very valuable link has been established with a local primary school. There are as many opportunities to lead assemblies as we are able to take up and, more recently, we have been able to establish a weekly after-school JAM (Jesus and Me) club for children in Years 5 and 6. There are, increasingly and encouragingly, overlaps with the work in school, the youth clubs and the annual holiday club.

Key to the development of church-family relationships and keeping a vision for the core has been our church weekend away, which is teaching based. It is heavily subsidised so that whole families can go and, for some, it is their only annual holiday. Special events such as a supper with a talk (meal provided free), Christian training weekends (Friday evening and Saturday morning) and a parish outreach every few years are added opportunities for teaching and evangelism.

Alongside this, it is very important for us to keep modelling evangelism and to have regular events which are easy to invite outsiders to—such as Mothering Sunday, when we issue special invitation cards. We now have more opportunities for evangelism and Bible teaching than we can handle.

Failures?

We have also tried many things that have been less successful. We did a door-to-door survey in a tough part of the estate. As a result of this 40 people indicated that they were interested to learn about the gospel. We hired a local community centre, put on tea and waited. Only one old man came. As a means of forming a group this venture failed, but it became a one-to-one Bible study and the man came to faith so, joy in heaven!

An Easter-tract letter-box drop in another area of the parish, when folk were invited to come and take a look at the claims of Jesus, brought only one unproductive response. These initiatives confirmed the lesson that personal/friendship evangelism is by far and away the best way to make progress and bring people under the sound of the gospel.

We have had many encouragements in the work at Walkergate but the pressures and problems do not go away! There is a constant pressure not to persevere with gospel proclamation and Bible-teaching ministry. Satan is ever at work seeking to undermine what God has said in His Word, but we must remember that there is no other way to do gospel ministry (1 Timothy 6 v 20-21; 2 Timothy 4 v 2-5). When results are small, when little appears to change and the progress is slow, discouragement seeps in. This problem is compounded by the fact that many of us were convert-ed in large churches, which has coloured our expectations. It is hard to keep preparing for small numbers, and resistance to the gospel is strong. Some do start well and then fall away, but we were warned of this in the Parable of the Sower.

The effects of this ministry are often long term. We long to see results now, so there must be a constant resolve to persevere and to exercise patience. It is easy to become lazy because Bible teach-ing and doing evangelism is a hard slog. It is far easier to get caught up in things that, unlike preparation and prayer, are more immediately rewarding and produce tangible results, eg: adminis-tration, visits and letter writing. It takes time to develop relation-ships, and perseverance and determination to go on preaching a message that people don't want to hear.

And then, if we are teaching the Bible faithfully, there will always be critics and criticism in the working-class situation can be pretty raw. We all like the praise of men but we need to remember that it's God's praise that counts. Sometimes our opponents leave and it's hard to bear—sometimes they don't, which is worse. Staleness is another problem, which creeps in as the years pass. It is easy to become bored, but gospel preparation and work will always be relentless. Added to this is the physical harshness of life in an urban situation: crime and grime! Much is grubby and bat-tered; constant vandalism and theft can grind down your spirits.

So how do we keep going in this type of situation? I hope these final pointers will provide a useful framework:

1. Don't lose your nerve on the gospel.

2. Be resolved to teach the Bible whatever comes.

3. Don't forget the privilege and joy of Christian ministry.

4. Keep in touch with godly friends.

And when the work is hard-going read 2 Corinthians 4 v 1-7.

Student ministry

Nathan Buttery

ONE OF THE MOST SIGNIFICANT BOOKS that I read in my days as a student was *In the Shadow of the Almighty* by Elizabeth Elliot. In it she chronicles the life of her husband Jim, as he went from being a student at Wheaton College in America to becoming a missionary among the (then unreached) people groups of Ecuador. It was to be a commitment that would cost him his life. During his time at university, Jim sought under God to get two degrees. First there was his academic degree, in which he excelled; second, and more important to him, there was what he called the 'AUG' the 'Approved Unto God' degree. That was to use the time at university to serve the God he loved with all his heart and not to waste a moment.

Jim's example was a great encouragement for me in seeking to make the most of my own student days, but continues to be so as I seek to minister among students. One's time as a student brings unparalleled opportunities for spiritual growth and evangelism, and in this sense, student ministry, while being no less or more important than any other type of ministry, does offer significant potential.

The principles of student ministry are the same as for any other type of ministry that seeks to disciple Christians. The text I refer to frequently is:

> [Jesus] we proclaim, warning everyone and teaching everyone with all wisdom, that we may present everyone mature in Christ.

For this I toil, struggling with all his energy that he powerfully works within me.' (ESV) **Colossians 1 v 28-29**

Student ministry is about proclaiming Christ and teaching Christ with the aim of producing mature Christians. And how do we do it? Working hard with the strength Christ gives. However, there are particular challenges that we face in seeking to minister to students in the 21st century. One is the increase of biblical illiteracy. This is, of course, a challenge that all of us face in whatever kind of ministry we are engaged in throughout Western Europe. But historically, it is true to say that changes and shifts in societal thinking are often to be found first in the universities and colleges. Christian foundations are being eroded, with very few students coming from what we might call 'Christian homes.'

Post-Christian students

In recent surveys that we have done on the Hull University campus, we found that of the hundreds of students we have interviewed, 80% claimed to be existentialist in their worldview. That means that a vast majority of students have no concept of absolute truth or morality, and so 'meaning', and 'purpose' is something you make up to get yourself through life. When pressed and shown the natural consequences of their belief, many students will simply shrug their shoulders and say: 'so what?'

It has horrified me in recent years to find some saying that Hitler was justified in doing what he did to 6 million Jews in the gas chambers! 'If there really is no such thing as absolute 'truth' who can argue with him?' Of course, pushing people to their logical extremes can backfire. I remember arguing with one woman student who was doing an MA in law and aiming to be a barrister. When I questioned how on earth she could do her job while not believing in absolute truth, she shouted at me and stormed off!

The trouble with such an intellectual climate is that it makes evangelism much more of a challenge. (Of course, it has always been tough!) With little or no biblical knowledge, and with so many more students coming from homes where the Bible is non-existent, we are starting from a position a lot further back. A few years ago, one could have confidence that most students were coming from a position of at least believing in God, even the God of the Bible—but that is a rarity nowadays. While not negating the miraculous intervention of God to bring someone to faith very quickly, and we have seen it happen, more often than not, for a student to come to faith requires, humanly speaking, a much longer period of time and a lot more patient biblical persuasion and proclamation.

The same may be said for students coming to university, who already call themselves Christians. While it is true to say that some will come from very good Bible-teaching churches and good Christian homes, sadly, the reality is that this is becoming less the case. Doctrinal confusion is rife and solid biblical nurturing is all too rare. Thus, nurture and discipleship of young Christian students must begin at a very basic level.

Furthermore, it raises the question of student leadership. If the trends continue, and of course we pray and work hard against that possibility, then Christian students coming to university will continue to have much less Christian experience and grounding. Is it therefore right to expect the same of students today in terms of leadership as we did even ten years ago? What is required is a much more hands-on approach, a patient nurturing of young men and woman, guiding them much more carefully in leadership.

The best leadership training I received was as I sat under godly men who showed me the ropes and gave me rope to hang myself with—but never allowing me to get that far! We need to seriously rethink our models of student ministry in response to the rapid decline in our Christian foundations.

Hostility

Coupled with this first challenge is another—the increasing hostility towards Christians on our campuses. As Christianity continues to be sidelined and ultimately removed from our national fabric, so hostility will grow. Societies which become more and more 'liberal' are supposed to become more and more 'tolerant'. However, the reality is that they are only tolerant to those they believe are tolerable. Opinions which were once deemed mainstream are now being pushed to the far right and labelled 'fundamentalist' (ie: no fun, all about damnation and decidedly mental!). This is seen all too often on the university campuses where evangelical Christianity is labelled 'extreme' and Christian Unions are excluded from Student Unions, or banned from meeting on Union property. We've experienced such hostility in Hull in the past, as have a number of other Christians Unions around the country. However, as I tell our students, this is no bad thing, since it teaches students at a young age to expect attack. Under God, such difficulties can galvanise young men and women to be the leaders and examples of the future.

A final challenge is the increasing financial pressure that many students are under today. It is well publicised that the average student will come out of education with more than £15,000 of debt—some with a lot more. This has had a number of effects on student ministry. One is that more students are taking paid work during their university careers in order to pay for their courses. This means that it is harder to encourage students to commit to discipleship courses and the like, because there is simply more pressure on their time. If they spend a day or two a week working just to make ends meet, then inevitably they have less time to serve and be involved in CU activities or local churches. A second consequence which I have begun to see is that more students are now deciding to live at home and commute to university on a daily basis to save money on rent. This is beginning to make us think seriously about how we lay on meetings and evangelistic events in the coming years.

A further consequence is the difficulty in attracting students to apprenticeship schemes after college. One of the big questions for many I speak to concerning working for a church or another organisation after university is: 'Will I be paid?' Often churches cannot afford to pay their workers at this level, and rely on home churches or families to support the workers. But if you are saddled with £15-20,000 of debt, then a one- or two-year apprenticeship is much less attractive, especially if your parents or bank manger are pressurising you to pay it back. We need to think of ways of ensuring that poorer churches and hard-up students can be freed up financially for service.

The greenhouse effect

While there are many challenges, student work still provides many joys. Two may be highlighted. One is what I call the 'Greenhouse Effect'. Given the challenges of living in post-Christian Britain, and the time pressures on students today, it is still true to say that great strides can be made, spiritually speaking, in a student's university career. It is like placing young men and women in a spiritual hothouse for three or four years. There is still time for in-depth study of God's Word and prayer. Personal discipleship can be done on a weekly basis with fewer time constraints than in later life. Conferences and study weekends can be attended. Friendships are fostered that will last a lifetime. University remains a wonderful opportunity to nurture young people in the faith. I think of one young man who came to university converted, yet poorly taught and not hugely enthusiastic. Yet, he now looks back on his time in university as a staggering period of growth, including tak-

The next obvious step...

Katie had been a Christian from the age of 8, but it was during her gap year in Bolivia with Latin Link that she first started reading her Bible, and 'got her act together' as a believer. 'I went to Nottingham University to study History, and thanks to all that God had taught me through his Word about what it means to be a disciple, I had already made lots of decisions about how I was going to live by the time I arrived.

'I discovered the CU straight away and, for the first time, I had lots of Christian friends. It was a shock to discover how untaught I was! Once I had got over my pride in working out how immature I was as a believer, I got stuck in and served on the CU committee in my final year.

'I really caught the CU vision for working with students from all denominations, so it was a really obvious choice to join the UCCF Relay scheme after I graduated. This is an apprenticeship scheme to train and disciple student workers. I got to do lots of talks and lead Bible studies, and got a real experience of what it's like to work as a full-timer. I then went to Portugal to work with IFES for a year with international students in Coimbra, north of Lisbon.'

Katie had a difficult choice to make after her return. 'Up to that time, I had just done the next most obvious thing. I loved student work, and seriously considered applying to work as a staff-worker for UCCF, but I was also keen to think about working overseas as well. So I decided to enrol for a PGCE at Nottingham, while continuing to help with the student work at my church.

'I would love to do full-time Christian work in the future, but I think it's right to get a teaching qualification now. If the way opens up for me go overseas, it will be extremely useful to have a professional qualification under my belt. Although fitting student work around a full-time job can be frustrating- I would love to be able to spend more time with individuals studying the Word—even so it is such a blessing to serve the Kingdom in this way'.

ing up a position in leadership which no one would have imagined when he first arrived—and continues to serve Christ today. His story can be multiplied many times over!

A second joy is the unparalleled evangelistic opportunities that university life offers. Given the challenges outlined above, this may seem a strange thing to say. But the fact remains that students are willing to talk and are open to the gospel. Christian students have contact with many more non-Christians than they will probably have in the future. They still largely live next to non-Christian colleagues in houses or halls of residence, rubbing shoulders day and night and able to share not only the gospel, but their lives as well. The university campus is one of the few places left where I can walk up to someone and instantly engage them in spiritual conversation without being ignored or thought weird (though the latter still happens!). Yes, students may be a lot further back spiritually speaking, yet they are still willing to talk.

Student ministry is, as with all ministry, a mixed bag. Many frustrations and many joys. How do we keep going? The text I frequently lay before my own team of helpers is:

> Therefore my beloved brothers, be steadfast, immovable, always abounding in the work of the Lord, knowing that in the Lord your labour is not in vain. **1 Corinthians 15 v 58**

While it has to be said that one feels like sometimes giving oneself rather half heartedly to the work of the Lord, yet the wonderful thing is that it is His work *and it is never in vain*. Let us never give up and let us strive, like Jim Elliot, for the ultimate approval: the AUG!

SECTION 3:
Getting from A to B

Guidance

Christopher Ash

HOW DO I KNOW THAT CHRIST HAS CALLED ME to 'prayer and the ministry of the Word'? How can I be sure?

I can't.

Not with the certainty for which I crave. (And if I think I can, I am probably self-deceived.) Rather, God gives us wisdom by His Spirit to know His character and general will (Colossians 1 v 9). And He gives us freedom to exercise that wisdom in making our choices. It is a mark of immaturity to expect to be told what to do in some more immediate way. And so chapters on guidance are always disappointing; because God is more concerned with our godliness than our guidance.

Jesus builds His church by giving gifts to His people

So, rather than start with ourselves, let's begin with the Lord Jesus Christ. He has promised to build His church (Matthew 16 v 18). He has died for her (Ephesians 5 v 25-26), been raised, and has ascended as the victor over 'him who has the power of death' (Hebrews 2 v 14). As the ascended conqueror He distributes His varied victory gifts to all His people (Ephesians 4 v 7-8), in order that His church shall be built up (1 Corinthians 12 v 7; 14 v 5; Ephesians 4 v 11-16). Every gift is needed, and no Christian is to despise any gift and think it useless (1 Corinthians 12 v 12-31). But we need to understand the distinct contribution to the church made by what we call 'Word' gifts.

'Word' gifts began with the apostles and prophets of the New Testament age, who were at the foundation of the church (Ephesians 2 v 20; 3 v 5). We have their unique and unchangeable testimony to the Lord Jesus in the New Testament. And then there are the ongoing 'Word' gifts, the evangelists (those who spread the good news, both to Christians and non-Christians), the pastors and teachers, who care for and lead God's church by preaching and teaching (Ephesians 4 v 11f). These are the equipping gifts; they equip all Christians to do the work of ministry with their own gifts, so that the church will be built up. So these 'Word' gifts have

---

Searching for a 'call'...

Ed worked for years as a teacher, and had many opportunities to share Christ at the school. But as his preaching opportunities grew, he started to wonder whether full-time ministry was a better option for him...

'Interestingly I have never felt I had a specific 'call' to full-time ministry, although I am sure I am doing what is wise and best.

'In making my decision I read several books—Spurgeon and Lloyd-Jones both state that one needs a definite 'call'. When I searched the Scriptures I could find no teaching for this (we are called to Christ, and to be holy, but what is a 'call' to be a teacher?...). Certainly men had been called to be apostles or prophets, but this 'narrative' doesn't imply that it should be the same for all.

'When I met with the church elders for the second time, they asked me if I was sure I had been called. I explained the above, and I said that (a) I thought I had been given the gifts necessary for being a pastor (and I think I have had the right experience for it), (b) I had a passion for pastoring, and (c) I thought it should be left to the elders to set me apart to be a pastor if, after seeking the Lord, they though it appropriate—this seemed to be the NT model.

The final decision went to the members of the whole church since they would need to support my wife and I. They decided to set me apart and train me—hallelujah! We've had our call—the church gave it to us.'

a special place in the Lord's church-building strategy. For without them other Christians will not be equipped for their ministries.

We must use the gifts He gives us for the building of His church

The most important principle to bear in mind here is very simple. It is the principle of *stewardship*. When the Lord Jesus has given us a gift, we must use it to build up His church (Romans 12 v 6; 1 Corinthians 12 v 7). This principle applies to all Christians, including those gifted as evangelists, pastors and teachers. On the last day, the Lord Jesus will ask us: 'What use did you make of the gifts I gave you?' (This is the principle in the parable of the talents, Matthew 25 v 14-30.) This principle of stewardship is very important. So the question is not, 'What do I want to do?' but rather, 'What am I gifted to do?'. As sinners we often want to do what we ought not to do, and we shy from doing what we ought to do.

There is little in scripture explicitly about the feelings or desires of the people set apart for Word ministry. When Paul speaks of those who aspire to the pastoral office (1 Timothy 3 v 1), he does not make it clear whether the candidates coming forward in Ephesus were to be encouraged or discouraged in their desire.

On the one hand, some desire to enter this ministry, and ought not to. They may, for example, have a wrong understanding of scripture (eg: 1 Timothy 1 v 7), a love of power (1 Peter 5 v 3) or prominence (3 John 9), a love of money (1 Timothy 6 v 5), or a desire to exploit vulnerable people by making them dependent upon them (2 Timothy 3 v 6f).

On the other hand, some want to avoid this ministry who ought to be in it, for pastoral ministry has its peculiar pressures. And so a love for the world (2 Timothy 4 v 10; 1 John 2 v 15-17), or a

'The last thing on earth I thought of doing'

Phil was born into a Christian family and spent many years resisting God (he would have called it 'seeking' at the time), before being converted at age 17. He went to study Chemistry at Imperial College, and taught secondary school science and maths for three years.

'At college, I went to a church that had a culture of 'gospel grafting'—they worked really hard to reach out for Christ. It was a lesson I learned well, and I had a desire to make an impact for the gospel. I started to help with a free-church camp, and discovered that many of the children, who had grown up in Christian homes, simply had no idea what the Bible actually says.

'So, with others, I started to produce some simple Bible notes for children. I wasn't really equipped to do this job. I wasn't a writer, or a designer. But the need was there, so I just got on with it, using whatever spare time I could find. And as I did these things, God helped me and blessed me, and the teaching gifts developed. A generous Christian offered to fund me to write some adult Bible notes full time, so for three years I worked away at it. At the end of that, I knew I wanted to give my life to gospel work. But I didn't know how. I had some opportunities to speak at camps, Bible classes, and so on, but I really did-n't think that preaching was for me.

'I went out to the Philippines for a couple of months to see if missionary work was something I should do. I pushed a few other doors too, but none of them seemed right. It was during this time that someone in the church said to me: 'Do you think you are called to preach?' I was, frankly, surprised at the sugges-tion, and a little reluctant when the people at my church started encouraging me in that direction. It was the last thing on earth I had thought of doing. I was shy, and not confident in front of people. I was much happier with a behind-the-scenes role. I guess they saw that God was already using me in teaching and personal work.

'After doing a year's training at a Bible college, I was invited to be the pastor of a small Grace Baptist church in South London, where I have ministered for the last twelve years.'

desire to avoid suffering (2 Timothy 1 v 6-12; cf. 1 Timothy 4 v 14) will make us avoid this work, even when we are called to it. So we must be deeply sceptical of our feelings and desires, for it is possible to quench the Spirit (1 Thessalonians 5 v 19).

So, rather than rely on our feelings, we do well to focus on the principles of stewardship. If Christ has given us 'Word' gifts, then we must use them, whether or not we want to. So the question resolves itself into asking: how will we discern whether we have these gifts? The New Testament answer may be summed up in three statements.

A. The gifts of Christ are discerned by the body of Christ as they are used by the servants of Christ.

The New Testament picture of a healthy church is one in which all believers are called to ministry (to be servants of Christ and His church). We are to throw ourselves wholeheartedly into doing what needs to be done. I am not to expect some prior revelation of my gifts, like a bank notification of a new PIN number, the envelope arriving secretly from heaven, so that I alone can scratch the paper to reveal my unique gift. Instead, I am to be an active servant. And as I serve, so the fellowships in which I serve will see what I am gifted at and what I am no good at. The latter experience may be painful, but is usually a part of the process.

I remember with some pain having to lead the singing at a school assembly unaccompanied (because the pianist was absent); it became rapidly evident that this was not my gift! We do not want *prima donnas* who will not volunteer to help, because 'this is not my gift'. Rather, we want servants who will have a go. So, if you are asked to help in some form of Christian service, say 'yes' if you possibly can. Have a go. And as you do, your brothers and sisters will tell you what you are gifted at and what you are not. They will help us 'think with sober judgement' about ourselves (Romans 12 v 3).

In particular, if you have opportunities to teach the Bible, to lead a Bible study, to give a talk at a summer venture or camp, or to preach in church, take these opportunities. Ask a mature Christian friend to watch and listen critically, and to give you (in love!) some honest feedback. Not to crush you (if you did badly) or flatter you (if you did well), but to help you see whether you have in bud a gift for Bible teaching.

A puzzling setback

'I became a Christian as a teenager, and took responsibility at the school CU and church youth group from an early age. I studied theology as a first degree, and started working life in publishing with a clear sense that I would end up 'in the ministry' at some stage.

'I took every opportunity to preach and teach. I ran a growing youth work at my church, and ran a big camp every summer. When I offered myself for training and ordination through the Anglican system, everyone, including me, thought that I would walk through the process, and that it was a 'done deal.'

'To everyone's surprise, the selection panel turned me down flat—a door closed so firmly and unexpectedly in my face that it made me re-assess my gifts, and the reasons why I had thought that I should follow this particular route in serving the Lord. Over the next few years, I continued to be actively involved in youth work, evangelism, preaching and teaching, and even looked at a few other options for full-time ministry. But none of them ever seemed quite right.

'Subsequently, through God's clear providence, I have been using my business, writing, teaching and preaching gifts through The Good Book Company which, we pray, will continue to be a blessing and support to many gospel workers throughout this country and the world. In God's wisdom, I now see, in part, why I received what, at the time, was a puzzling and painful setback. God clearly had other plans for my life.'

Incidentally, let us beware of replacing 'gifts' with 'strategy' in our thinking. We love to plan our lives, to ask and answer the question: 'Where will I be of most use to Christ?' It is a fine question. But only the Lord knows the answer. And it is probably not the answer of our strategising, in which we are in control. We like to plan a life of maximal 'effectiveness', but this is not in our power.

B. Church leaders should appoint to Word ministries those in whom they recognise Word gifts

Leaders are better equipped than we to recognise the gifts and calling of God. They watch our characters, listen to our teaching, see how we relate to others and how we respond under pressure. This is why the responsibility for the leaders of the future lies with the leaders of the present. Paul was subjectively convinced of his call by Christ to be an apostle, and the collective leadership of the church recognised this particular grace given to him, to be the apostle to the Gentiles (Galatians 2 v 8f).

The leadership in Antioch heard and recognised the call of Christ by His Spirit to Saul and Barnabas to cross-cultural mission (Acts 13 v 1-3). They, in turn, appointed elders (Acts 14 v 23), as did Titus in Crete later (Titus 1 v 5). Paul and the collective eldership recognised the gift in Timothy; when they laid hands on him they did not confer gifts upon him (as if they were the priestly purveyors of grace) but rather recognised the gifting of the Lord Jesus Christ (1 Timothy 4 v 14; 2 Timothy 1 v 6). And then, Timothy in his turn, is to look out for faithful people to whom he can entrust the message (2 Timothy 2 v 2).

As Christian leaders seek the next generation of ministers of the Word, they will look for four qualities.

1. A godly character

They will look first for men and women of godly character. 'If anyone aspires to the office of overseer, he desires a noble task. Therefore an overseer must be...' (1 Timothy 3 v 1-3, ESV). The logic of the 'therefore' is that because this is a noble task, the qualifications for it must be rigorously maintained. The 'checklists' in 1 Timothy 3 v 1-7 and Titus 1 v 5-9 are overwhelmingly moral. Others will judge this better than us. For if we think we are godly, it is a sure sign we are not. Rather, their judgement will need to overcome our own reluctance (cf. James 3 v 1-12).

2. A clear gospel

Allied with godly character, they will look for a clear and tenacious grasp of the gospel of the Lord Jesus. We must have a clear grasp of this message. But it is not enough to understand it. To be a pastor, we must hold to it tenaciously, be willing not only to teach it positively but also to correct those who teach in error (Titus 1 v 9). We must be prepared to face opposition and suffer for the name of the Lord Jesus.

3. The ability to teach

Twice in the pastoral letters, one quality is mentioned that stands out from the rest: the ability to teach (1 Timothy 3 v 2; 2 Timothy 2 v 24). The same quality is implied in Titus 1 v 9, where the elder 'must be able to give instruction in sound doctrine and also to rebuke those who contradict it' (ESV).

The other qualities listed ought to be true of every Christian. But not this one. A deeply godly believer may not have this ability. And yet, without this ability, it is disastrous for someone to enter pastoral ministry. For this is the ministry of the Word, and therefore suitable only for those who can understand and handle words. So when we interview candidates for the Cornhill Training

Course we look for some evidence of an ability to teach the Bible. Often this gifting is only evident in bud; but it must be there.

4. A love for people

Lastly, they will look for a love for people, for teaching is more than explanation. It is relational, just as God's revealed truth is the relational expression of divine love. No teacher will be heard unless he loves the people he teaches. Paul speaks of the ability to teach in the context of a teacher who is gentle when provoked, prayerful when opposed, and driven by a longing to win his hearers back to God (2 Timothy 2 v 14-26). Without this love for people, the clearest and cleverest Bible scholar in the world is not able to teach.

C. The path to 'Word ministry' takes time and testing

We live in a very hurried culture. We want to know now what is the calling of Christ for the rest of our lives. But callings to Christian ministry are to be tested over time (eg: 1 Timothy 3 v 10 for deacons, and 5 v 22 for elders). The main reason for this is that character only becomes evident over time. A church leader who lays hands on someone in haste will often have to repent at leisure (1 Timothy 5 v 22).

One of the most encouraging developments in biblical Christianity in the UK in recent years has been the growth of 'testing paths' by which Christians can, as it were, dip their toes in the waters of Word ministry, so that together we may gradually discern whether or not this is their gift. The path I am most familiar with is the Cornhill Training Course, and in particular the option of doing our Cornhill Ministry Scheme, by which students take the Cornhill course two days a week for two years, while being apprenticed by a local church the rest of the week. This scheme has been replicated throughout the country in numerous, similar local training schemes run by local Gospel Partnerships. They combine a rigorous training in handling the Bible with plenty of 'hands on' ministry at the sharp end of local church life. But there are many other excellent options (see the chapter on training). If you think Christ may have gifted you for this Word ministry, pursue one of these 'toe in the water' options if you can.

Although we have seen that our desires are an unreliable indicator of Christ's gifts, nevertheless you will expect to find in your

---

'The best job in the world...'

Pete can't put a finger on when, precisely, he was converted. 'At the age of 17, I went on a summer youth camp and heard the Bible taught in a way I'd not heard before, and I wanted more. When the time came for me to go to university, I chose Newcastle-upon-Tyne—partly because that was where the leader of the youth camp had recently started leading a church.

'As I sat under this teaching ministry, and got involved in the church as a student, I started to understand things that I thought I knew but clearly didn't! Before this time, I would have said: 'Christianity is important.' But now everything took on a much greater profile: I began to understand the importance of the gospel and the importance of ministry. After university, I worked as a pastoral assistant at the church for a year.

'It was a fantastic year, but in some ways it put me off! I observed the relentless pressure of gospel ministry, and the huge responsibility of faithfully teaching God's Word to people week in, week out. I guess I was a little frightened by it. I moved to London and worked as a designer for three years while getting increasingly involved in my local church—teaching the youth group with a bit of adult preaching thrown in. During that time I was encouraged by both my church in London and the minister in Newcastle to consider full-time ministry.

'I loved my job and the people I worked with, but I recognised the enormous need for gospel workers. I decided to apply for training in the Church of England. It was a 'win-win' situation. If I got accepted I would get to do the best job in the world; if I didn't, then I loved the job I was doing. In the end I was accepted for training and have not looked back.'

heart some Spirit-given echo of the heart longing of the Lord Jesus for His sheep (Matthew 9 v 36; John 21 v 15-17). We must expect that the desire of church leaders to set you apart for this work will be answered by a willingness in your heart to be appointed, for this ministry must be done from a willing heart. It is not to be done 'under compulsion, but willingly, as God would have you (do it)' (1 Peter 5 v 2). I may or may not want to do it, in the shallow sense that I may want to go on a Caribbean holiday, to give me pleasure, self-fulfilment and delight. But I must be willing to do it.

There is perhaps an analogy with the comparison between a Western marriage, in which the bridegroom chooses the bride, and some cultures in which the parents arrange the marriage. In each case, the critical point is that, however the bridegroom comes face to face with the bride, he must consent to marry her. It does not, in the last analysis, matter whether he himself has taken the initiative to propose to her, or his parents have negotiated the match. What matters is that *he is willing*, he consents to marry her (and of course, she him!). So with pastoral ministry. It doesn't matter whether the initiative began with me, or began with church leaders. In the end, I must be willing to serve in this way.

Conclusion: you are free to decide!

Finally, remember wisdom and freedom. You are free as a Christian to make your own decisions with the wisdom God gives you. You must neither let yourself be pressured into pastoral ministry by pushy leaders, nor dissuaded by worldly motives. You must decide. It is before your own Master you stand or fall; and He is able to make you stand. The rest of us will not sit in judgement upon your decision.

No principles in this chapter will make your decision for you. You decide; and as you decide, the Lord Jesus Christ is working out

His purposes, fulfilling His promise to build His church. And so the glory will be His alone.

Apprenticeships
Ian Garrett

IMAGINE YOU WANTED TO BECOME A PLUMBER. Somewhere along the way, you'd serve an apprenticeship alongside an experienced plumber. You'd learn by watching him and asking questions. You'd learn by doing things yourself and being watched. You'd learn by making mistakes and being bailed out. Doubtless some book work and exams would come into it, but the heart of working out whether you really wanted to be a plumber, and of becoming one, would be an apprenticeship.

When you look to the New Testament for how to do gospel ministry, you find the same model. For example, Paul wrote to those who became Christians through him in Philippi: 'Whatever you have learned or received or heard from me, or seen in me—put it into practice' (Philippians 4 v 9). So the Philippians watched Paul's life and ministry, caught his vision and priorities—and then both copied him in Philippi (Philippians 1 v 27-30) and supported him once he'd moved on (Philippians 4 v 15-16). So Paul thanked God for their 'partnership in the gospel' (Philippians 1 v 5): it's as if he'd 'apprenticed' them into the 'business' of gospel ministry.

But you see that model of apprenticeship, not just in how Paul brought on Christians to maturity, but in how he brought on 'full-time ministers'. For example, Acts 16 v 1-5 tells how Paul took on Timothy, as a companion on a missionary journey. Later, writing to the Philippians, he could say: 'But you know that Timothy has proved

himself, because as a son with his father [the most common apprenticeship in those days—a son picking up his father's business] he has
served with me in the work of the gospel.' (Philippians 2 v 22).

The previous chapter (on guidance) mentioned opportunities
for testing out whether full-time ministry might be for you. And

---

'A real privilege...'

Andy became a Christian at university, but had no clear career ideas after deciding to quit teacher training. 'I drifted into a 9-to-5 job, and was working hard,
and trying to get involved in my local church. I'd been at the church for a year
and a half before the minister said to me: 'Would you like to become an apprentice'. I was both surprised and honoured and it sounded like a good idea. I'd
seen the other guys who were doing the job, and thought it would be a real privilege to be given the time and space to study the Bible in depth. I didn't know
exactly what was involved, but I was hungry at that stage for teaching, and it
came at the right time. It wasn't a hard decision for me, because I had little to
give up and everything to gain.

I studied part time at at a Bible college, and helped to head up the 20s and 30s
meeting on Sunday evening; I also co-led a Bible-study group for new Christians.
The work included a lot of catering which was good fun, and I also had some
practical responsibilties as head caretaker—making sure the church building was
ready for Sundays.

'I also got my first chance to do some preaching. The first time in the pulpit, I
was absolutely terrified—but then, and every time since, God has taken away the
fear and given me some degree of fluency.

'College was wonderful and really moved me on spiritually—but the staff meetings were also very important. I think I learnt more at them, just by listening,
about the priorities and practicalities of the Christian life and local church leadership. Halfway through my training it dawned on me that I had been given so
much, so it would be a crime not to use the understanding and skills I'd developed, and that I would love to do some kind of Word and prayer ministry. I started out on the apprenticeship thinking that I would go back into secular work,
but now, if at all possible, I'd love to do full-time Christian work.'

they're basically apprenticeships. For example, in the church I serve, we have six apprentices in a paid, one- or two-year role, in which they work alongside full-time ministers. So this chapter is about the what, why, who, when and how of apprenticeships.

What and why?

What is an apprenticeship in gospel ministry and why do one? Apprenticeships offer at least four vital opportunities:

1. To see ministry from the inside

Many of us, when considering full-time ministry, have little idea of what it really involves. Some of us may only have been part of the youth, student or young professionals side of a church. But as an apprentice, you get to see the whole thing—from the vital role of a crèche in freeing parents to be in church, through to the vital responsibility of caring for elderly, housebound saints.

Again, some of us may see full-time ministry as largely the (apparently) glamourous role of giving talks. But as an apprentice, you see how full-time ministers must 'discharge all the duties of [their] ministry' (2 Timothy 4 v 5)—ie: that it's more than just giving talks. And watching me, for example, struggling over sermon preparation and having to stay up late at it, will give apprentices a less glamourous, more realistic, view of the 'Word' side of ministry. Over time, they'll see those of us who are full-timers facing all sorts of opportunities, problems, joys and discouragements in ministry—as well as facing their own. And all the time they can be asking questions of us: 'How should I follow up someone who's dropped out of church?'; 'How do you organise your prayer for ministry?'; 'Why do we do that in Sunday services?'; and so on.

2. To do ministry and be stretched further

Apprentices have already been doing ministry before they join us —for example, personal evangelism, leading Bible studies and one-to-ones, leading youth work or camps. In fact, the ministry people have already done is a major factor in discerning whether they should do an apprenticeship.

What an apprenticeship then offers is the opportunity to do more ministry and be stretched further. The aim is to help apprentices make progress in ministries they've already been doing, and to help them start and develop in new ministries (eg: giving talks, leading leaders). Embryonic gifts of Bible-handling and leadership can be tested over time. And the fundamental quality of servant-hood (Mark 10 v 42-45) can be tested over the photocopier, mopping the floor, or setting out chairs.

3. To be trained in ministry

Although we run formal training sessions for our apprentices, 'training' is far wider than that. For example, it's training when our apprentices get feedback on their talks; or as they sit in on meetings planning a 10-year strategy for the church; or when we cross paths at coffee time and talk about the things we're preparing. In fact, God's training of us (eg: Hebrews 12 v 4-13) is wider even than that: we're trained by all our experience—from being ill, to no-one turning up to an evangelistic event.

But we do lay on formal training. For example, our apprentices get a day a week of seminars and personal study. Over two years we look at: a Bible overview; Mark; Romans; an Old Testament book; systematic theology; and church history. We cover: principles of understanding and applying the different parts of the Bible; skills of how to teach it in different forms of Word ministry; and wider skills—from time management to leadership. At the same time, each of our apprentices has one-to-one supervision—to oversee their ministry and encourage their growth in faith and Christlikeness. Apprenticeships vary from place to place. But the common aim is to develop those things we saw in 1 Timothy 3 v 1-13 in the chapter on guidance: conviction about the Bible; a Christlike character; and competence in teaching and leadership.

Now, any formal training at apprenticeship stage (typically one or two days' study and teaching a week) will, for many ministries, not be a sufficient foundation for a lifetime's work. There are many different ministries (1 Corinthians 12 v 4-6) even among full-timers – eg: the ministry of a pastor-teacher responsible for overall congregational teaching and the ministry of a women's worker doing largely 'one-to-one' or small group work. And those different ministries require different levels of training. But some—eg: the ministry of the overall pastor-teacher—will require a far more substantial, foundational training in the Bible than an apprenticeship can offer (see the next chapter on theological education).

An apprenticeship should ideally offer some formal training, but, perhaps more importantly, it will show you what you need training for. Many people now in full-time ministry can testify that time spent as an apprentice helped them understand what they needed training for—and therefore helped them to choose a college and course wisely, and motivated them for sticking at hard study. For example, a former co-worker of mine, who has just been through Bible college, told me he stuck at learning New Testament Greek, partly because he'd seen how often I used it when we were trying to sort out together what a tricky Bible passage meant.

4. To be watched in ministry by older ministers

As we saw in the chapter on guidance, the responsibility for discerning and training the leaders of the future lies with the leaders of the present. The model in 1 Timothy 3 v 1-13 is that Timothy is to be watching out for future leaders—watching for people showing the convictions, character and competence that point to their taking on more ministry. And one of the most important things an apprenticeship offers is that opportunity to be watched by an older minister (or ministers), who can then play a major part in evaluating your suitability for full-time ministry.

An early 'apprenticeship' for me was my gap year. I worked with a missionary couple in Kenya. They watched me give my first Bible talks, oversee the school Christian Union and set up Bible studies

---

'I discovered what I'm best at...'

James was 'doing well' as a charity fund raiser, but every wedding he went to made him angry. 'I kept hearing terrible talks and wasted gospel opportunities from ministers, and I thought: "I could do better than this." But when my minister first suggested that I do an apprenticeship, I ran a mile. I was scared about the drop in salary, my own poor understanding and what my family would think.'

'But I was wrestling with the idea and felt convinced that I should do it, to see if it was right for me or not. When I signed up as an apprentice, I was right about my family's reaction—my mum thought I had joined a cult and cried for days; and my dad gave me a serious grilling and thought the whole thing "unwise."

'The apprenticeship involved lots of administration running a lunchtime ministry. I also helped lead evangelistic courses, and gave some talks. I enjoyed many aspects of the work, but found the whole process of preparing and writing talks painful and difficult. I would often be awake at midnight, desperate and irritable, trying to give some shape to what I had to say.

'Everyone has strengths and weaknesses, including ministers, but it slowly became clear to me that the one weakness that a minister can't have is in teaching and preaching. When I thought about other areas of work, I would spark with ideas and enthusiasm, but preaching left me twitching and nervous! My time as an apprentice was terrific. I ended the year knowing that full-time Word ministry, certainly for the time being, was not for me. But I had also become convinced that I wanted to stay in Christian work of some kind.'

for the boys. They watched me for a year; then, towards the end, they sat me down and said: 'Did you realise you had these gifts? We think, having watched you, that you should be praying about whether this is how you can best serve the Lord in the long-term.' That was very significant for me: we rightly hesitate to think we have the gifts for ministry; we're rightly wary of putting ourselves forward—which is why we need the judgement and objectivity of older ministers to evaluate our gifts and all the other things mentioned in 1 Timothy 3 v 1-13. And one of the main purposes of an apprenticeship is that, by the end of it, older ministers can help you answer the question: 'Should I pursue full-time ministry, or should I serve the Lord in a different walk of life?'

Who and when?

Who should consider an apprenticeship in gospel ministry, and when?

Let me say straight away that a full-time, paid apprenticeship in gospel ministry is not a necessity on the pathway towards full-time ministry. For example, a friend of mine became an engineer after graduating and settled into a local church. He led men's evangelism, was given regular, supervised opportunities to preach and became one of the church elders. And his pastor invested a good deal of time in him. And those three years, although not a full-time, paid apprenticeship, were his proving ground—which led him, ultimately, to Bible college and on into full-time ministry.

But, for many, a full-time, paid apprenticeship has been an important step on the way. The people I most encourage to consider doing one are those for whom the question: 'Might full-time ministry be for me?' is at the front of their minds. When we interview applicants, we ask them why they want to do an apprenticeship. Sometimes they say things like, 'To grow as a Christian', or

'To serve the church,' or 'To learn more about the Bible.' All good aims, but the point is that any healthy Christian ought to be wanting those things—and can do them without becoming a full-time, paid apprentice.

I'm not saying that you have to be pretty well certain that full-time ministry might be for you—after all, moving towards or away from that conclusion is part of what an apprenticeship is about. I'm simply saying that apprenticeships are of particular value to the person for whom that question is at the front of the mind. But at our church, we take on apprentices who vary a good deal in their thinking about future possibilities. For example, some of the men are wondering about the possibility of being a life-long pastor-teacher; whereas some of the women, with less obvious ministry pathways, are just thinking two years ahead with a range of possibilities (Christian or secular work) beyond that.

Paul wrote to Timothy, on appointing future leaders: 'He must not be a recent convert, or he may become conceited and fall under the same judgment as the devil' (1 Timothy 3 v 6). So there's a danger of doing 'too much too soon'. For example, I've seen students converted in their second year, who've grown fast as Christians, but for whom it would have been 'too much too soon' to become an apprentice immediately after graduating. That's a question of judgement for which you'll need the help of older ministers who know you (and of any who interview you for an apprenticeship).

It also needs saying that apprenticeships are not just for those who've just graduated—nor just for those who've been through university. I know a variety of people in their twenties and thirties who've done one. It can be more difficult later on, eg: there may be financial implications, especially if married with children (some apprenticeships provide a grant; others require you to raise some or all of your own support). But God is sovereign over any situations where doing one earlier may not have been possible or wise.

How?

Finally, how can you find an apprenticeship? The first thing to say is: talk to the older ministers who know you best. There may be opportunities in the church to which you currently belong. That has the advantage of continuity of relationships, which is good for ministry and also means you're being watched by those who have a head-start in knowing you. But you may have to look elsewhere —again, seek the help of older ministers around you.

Apprenticeships vary from being quite general (doing a bit of everything) to being more specialist (eg: majoring on youth or student work). So your choice may be affected by whether your heart is in a particular area of ministry. They also vary as to how much formal training they offer, whether there is just one apprentice or a small peer-group, and what kind of church context they're in (eg: university town, inner city, rural, or overseas). There are also apprenticeships in 'parachurch' organisations, eg: those working among students. They offer a good number of the same ministry experiences, but lack the opportunity to grapple in-depth with local-church ministry—which is very valuable for those considering whether that might be God's will for them in the long-term. (A number of people I know have done a 'parachurch' apprenticeship one year and then a church-based one the next.)

There are a growing number of apprenticeships, and you may find yourself investigating several and choosing which to apply for. That creates the danger of 'consumer thinking' and asking merely: 'What will I get out of this?' (What training, opportunities, financial support?) Whereas the Lord Jesus said: 'For even the Son of Man did not come to be served, but to serve and to give his life as a ransom for many' (Mark 10 v 45). If you're a Christian, then above all, you're apprenticed to the Lord who said that. And if you're to be an apprentice in a church or Christian organisation, you're to come to it not with the attitude: 'What will I get out of it?', but with the attitude: 'What can I give, and how can I serve?'

Where might an apprenticeship lead?

If God does guide you into an apprenticeship, there are three possible outcomes at the end:

1. Encouragement from those who've been watching you to press on towards full-time ministry straight away (and advice about what pathway to pursue).

2. Encouragement to press on towards full-time ministry—but not yet: it may be that those watching you think you need to do some more growing up, or get some more experience outside full-time ministry.

3. Encouragement to conclude that full-time ministry is not for you. That doesn't mean you're in any way 'second class' or left with 'second best' in life: God made you and is sovereign over your gifts and temperament and what you are, and aren't, cut out for. If, after doing an apprenticeship, you conclude that full-time ministry isn't for you, that's a vital step towards clarifying what is. And time spent as an apprentice will not have been wasted, but will send you out better equipped to be a witness in the world and to play your part, in partnership with full-timers, in the church.

Finding apprenticeships

Visit the 9:38 website for a list of apprenticeship opportunities, and further information on how to go about finding an apprenticeship position. www.ninethirtyeight.org

Training for ministry

David Peterson

WHEN PAUL GAVE HIS FAREWELL address to the Ephesian elders
(Acts 20 v 18-35), he first drew attention to his own example as a
pastor in their midst: 'serving the Lord with all humility and with
tears and with trials' (v 19). Trials came through the opposition of
unbelievers, but tears came from three years of admonishing
believers to lead lives worthy of the gospel (v 31). Paul's sacrificial
service to the Lord was also demonstrated in his desire to avoid
any hint of covetousness, and so he worked to supply his own
practical needs and the needs of others (v 33-35). Although he
wrote about the right of gospel workers to be supported financially (1 Cor 9 v 13-14; Gal 6 v 6-10), he himself did not always take
advantage of that right. Paul's Christ-like example was also set
before the elders as he spoke about his willingness to suffer impris-
onment and affliction for the sake of the gospel (v 22-4).

So Paul commended his own model of leadership to the
Ephesians, as part of his strategy for encouraging them to be faithful and effective in the future. At the same time, he spoke about
the breadth and depth of his teaching ministry. There was no
shrinking from declaring the truth to them, no matter what the
cost to him personally (v 20, 27). Every opportunity was taken for
public and private teaching. Somewhat surprisingly, Paul highlighted repentance and faith first (v 21), even though these are the
outcome or final appeal of the gospel. However, he clearly set this
appeal within the context of expounding the gospel of grace (v 24,
32). Two other terms then describe the wider biblical framework

he gave to them: 'the kingdom' (v 25) and 'the whole counsel of God' (v 27). Like the Lord Jesus, he sought to show how the whole Bible pointed to, and prepared for, the coming of the Saviour, His death and resurrection, and the proclamation of the gospel to all nations (Luke 24 v 25-7, 44-49).

Paul did not simply preach the gospel to unbelievers. He continued to teach the gospel and its implications to Christians. He did this by opening the Scriptures to them in the light of their fulfilment in Christ. But we know from his sermons in Acts and from the teaching in his letters that this involved more than text-proofing to make believers feel good about themselves and God! He showed them how the will or plan of God for the whole created order is fulfilled in the Lord Jesus. As he proclaimed the grace of God to them, he continued to explore the deeper, everyday implications of 'repentance towards God and of faith in our Lord Jesus Christ' (Acts 20 v 21), admonishing them night or day with tears (v 31).

As he left them to go to Jerusalem and the distress that awaited him there, Paul challenged the elders to preserve the church in truth and holiness (v 26-28). He predicted that fierce wolves would come in from the outside to destroy the flock, and that false teaching could even arise from the body of elders itself (v 29-30). Only God and the message of his grace would be adequate to build the church, to bring every member safely into the inheritance promised by God, and to enable believers to live meanwhile as the sanctified people of God (v 32).

Responding to the challenge

Paul gives us a holistic picture of leadership, which is remarkably relevant to our situation today. If you are considering the possibility of full-time Christian ministry, it may well be because of the example of a godly pastor, whose model you want to follow. You have experienced the benefits of such leadership and you want to see it extended and multiplied, for the sake of others and for the glory of the Lord Jesus Christ. How can you train to be more like the sort of pastor Paul exemplified?

Most obviously, try and work with an effective leader in a church context, asking questions, observing, reflecting, and putting into practice what you learn. Apprenticeships before any formal theological education are a vital opportunity for this. But it is also important to keep that practical learning going, even in a reduced fashion, during a period of more academic engagement, to enable theory and practice to interact. Ideally, further experience as a member of a ministry team should then precede any acceptance of ultimate responsibility in Christian work.

But why consider formal theological education? Isn't on-the-job learning more valuable, especially if the pastor you work with is a good teacher? Isn't full-time theological education an unnecessary luxury? Haven't people lost their zeal and vision through becoming too academic? Don't theological colleges 'kill the church'?

Such questions are often asked and I want to try and answer them in reverse order. It is true that some theological education is directly responsible for killing the church. A purely academic approach, coupled with cynicism about the teaching of Scripture and its authority, can destroy enthusiasm for evangelism and biblical teaching. There are probably many denominational leaders today whose liberal theology and ethics were formed by the sort of training they received. Far from encouraging gospel ministry and church growth, they often set themselves against those who would promote these things. But theological education does not have to be destructive like that. Everything depends on the ethos of the course, its content, how it is taught, and by whom.

Gaining depth for the long-term...

From the age of about 15, Nathan had expressed a desire to serve the Lord in his local church. 'They got me reading books, and started to help me test my gifts, but encouraged me not to dive into full-time ministry before I had got some life experience and matured as a Christian. It was wise advice. So I stayed at home, got an apprenticeship as an electronics engineer, and progressed in my work while getting greater and greater experience of practical ministry in the church and life experience in general.

'By my mid 20s, I was preaching regularly, leading a homegroup and running the youth group with another couple, and was married with one child. After speaking again with the church leaders I was encouraged to train for full-time ministry, and applied for a church apprenticeship. The minister who interviewed me helped me see that the experience I had already gained in my local church would only be repeated in the apprenticeship, and that I should consider Bible college instead. My church agreed.

'I was worried about raising the money for college and to support my family. With the backing of my church, I wrote a letter round to friends and relations, and places that I had preached. God provided for us amazingly, and we signed up to go to a theological college for three years.

'I was quite nervous about it. I'd not been to university before, and I always considered myself a practical person, rather than an academic. I also had a suspicion that, somehow, three years out of ministry was a bit of a waste of time; why spend all that time in a library when I could be preaching and getting on with the work? It seemed to defeat the object. However after one amazing year here, I can now see why that thinking is wrong. (Even for a non-academic like me.)

'It *is* possible to learn 'on the hoof' in ministry, but the pressure of preparing and preaching regularly means that there is a danger of what you preach being all that you know. Having three years here will give a depth to my ministry that I wouldn't have the time and space, or possibly the encouragement, to pursue if I was serving in a church. Like many people, I believed things because of my church background. Meeting people with a variety of views on secondary issues has helped me to examine the basis of why I held to certain things. The fellowship with students and staff here has been amazing, and I have learned so much through the lectures, informal conversations and hearing others give talks.'

Far from being a luxury, biblically-driven theological education is vital for the life of the church and for the development of its mission. There are parts of the world today where evangelism is taking place at a great rate, many are being converted and congregations are being planted on a regular basis. But there are few pastors in these regions who receive anything beyond basic training, and leaders are crying out for more theological educators to help mature the churches.

When people in countries like the United Kingdom call for a minimal approach to theological education, they are not being realistic about the culture in which they live, and seem to have an idealistic view about the way Christianity can flourish without well-trained leadership. We require school teachers to have degrees in their subject, but some seem unwilling to apply this standard to the teaching of God's Word. We live in a context where more and more people benefit from tertiary education, where the media, the politicians, and intellectuals in many spheres challenge the Christian worldview. Pastors need to be well trained to equip the saints for ministry in such a world (Ephesians 4 v 11-16). Believers need to be taught how to recognise and resist error, and to make a defence to anyone who asks them to give a reason for the hope they have (1 Peter 3 v 15).

You can begin to see the value and importance of good training institutions when you consider the limits of on-the-job learning, even with someone who is an excellent teacher. Three years of daily contact with the apostle Paul, hearing him lecture in the hall of Tyrannus (Acts 19 v 9), and observing him engaged in evangelism and the nurture of believers, must have been a marvellous experience for the Ephesian elders. But is there an individual who can offer such training today? Potentially, the strength of a theological college or seminary is the team of gifted teachers, each of whom is an expert in a different field, combining their gifts to offer the sort of holistic learning indicated by the apostle in Acts 20. It is not possible for most people to be competent in all the areas that are involved in effective theological education. Specialisation in biblical studies, or the historical and theological disciplines, or pastoral training, is usually necessary. Engaging with such a team, students can have a period of concentrated study and reflection, away from the daily pressures of ministry, but not divorced from pastoral experience.

Some, however, would argue for the benefit of private study, either through a correspondence course or the kind of university education that gives you lots of time to read and write essays and to do ministry on the side. Correspondence courses are great up to a certain level, and self-education through reading and supervised assessments has its value as well. But an education that is truly biblical, and formative for Christian leadership, will involve interaction with others in a fellowship of learning and corporate worship (Colossians 3 v 16; Hebrews 3 v 13; 10 v 24-25). It will involve exposure to the gifts and ministries of many others and the opportunity to share with them what you are learning (Romans 12 v 3-8). Scripture does not encourage an individualistic approach to learning and growth to maturity in Christ, and neither should we.

Not everyone may be able to afford full-time theological education in a residential context. However, the benefits are such that each person seeking training for Christian leadership should seek to spend as much time as is possible in such an environment. Those who are married should reflect also on the benefit for their family, if they can join in the experience of residential training, learning and growing with others who are heading for similar ministries together. It may be necessary to remain at home and commute, but some involvement of the family in the life of the theological institution is desirable. Those who are in a position to finance the training of potential pastors and teachers, youth and children's workers, cross-cultural missionaries and evangelists, should do their utmost to ensure that training is not limited because of a lack of funding.

What to look for in a training institution

A colleague of mine has rightly argued that effective training for gospel ministry can be summed up in three words: knowledge, skills, and personal formation.

You need to have the necessary knowledge and skills to apply the Bible, entailing **exegesis** (how to understand texts), **hermeneutics** (how to interpret those texts), and the appropriate skills for delivering the Bible's message to your particular context. You need to understand how the church, guided by the Holy Spirit, has wrestled with these issues through history. You need a sensitive and robust **systematic theology**, so that you can make sense of the all the biblical data. You need to be able to **understand people** and the contexts in which they live, so that you can minister to them more effectively. And, above all, you need to be fashioned as a man or woman into one who is **godly and prayerful**, whose gifts are not exercised except with a servant heart.

Find out what knowledge and skills are being offered by the institution you are investigating, and ask how they propose to help you in your personal formation for Christian ministry. Look at the faculty profiles and discover their areas of expertise and experience. Check out the resources of the institution, especially the library, accommodation and study facilities. What opportunities do they give for practical on-the-job learning? But, above all, pay careful attention to the contents and structure of the course, its compulsory and optional elements, and how the various strands integrate and hold together.

In the biblical studies area, consider how much emphasis is placed on learning and using the biblical languages. Not everyone will be able to master Greek and Hebrew, but an institution that takes biblical interpretation seriously will encourage as many as possible to achieve the highest level of competence in one or both languages. This should enable students to evaluate different English translations, to work directly from the original text to

A poor choice

'When my church sent me for training, we chose a Bible college that had a good reputation in the evangelical world, and had a lot of overseas students. It turned out to be a great disappointment.

'I came from a church where I had been well taught, and, although I couldn't put all the pieces together, I just knew that the teaching was wrong. There were some great and godly people at the college, but the main lecturer was an open theist—although I couldn't put that name to it at the time—and I soon saw that this thinking influenced virtually every area of study. Most of the students were from overseas and came from a much less solid background. I was amazed how easily they were taken in. We were meant to be strengthened and trained, but, sadly, many came out more confused than when they arrived.

'He seemed trendy, modern and daring in a way that made traditional evangelicalism seem boring, hidebound and conservative. So in virtually every lecture I spent time arguing with him. It was a difficult time.

'Eventually, I realised that it was doing bad things to me—to my head and my heart! If I stayed there, I would come out wanting to fight everyone, not to save everyone. So after the first year I left and joined a different course with a very clear focus on the Bible—it was like heaven by comparison! In one sense I really grew from the testing—it pushed me to think through what I believe—but then I could very easily have gone off the rails.'

understand a biblical writer's emphases and allusions, to use commentaries with discernment, and to establish a structure for preaching from the text itself. Biblical studies modules should be committed to teaching an integrated biblical theology. This will mean explaining how the different parts of the Bible relate to one another, how the saving plan of God is progressively revealed and worked out, and how Jesus Christ is the fulfilment of that plan. Such an approach will encourage you to respond to the Old Testament from a Christian perspective (cf. 2 Timothy 3 v 14-17), not simply treating it as a history of Israel or as a handbook of Jewish theology.

Effective theological training will also involve a study of church history, to discover how the Christian mission developed at different times and in different contexts, and to see how great doctrinal and pastoral issues were resolved. There is much to be learned from the past, and it is inhibiting not to have a grasp of the whole span of church history, or a specialised knowledge of an era of special importance such as the Reformation of the sixteenth century. It is also important to develop a systematic theology, so that you can synthesize the biblical data and evaluate it in the light of the great debates of the past. Such study is a vital step towards the application of Scripture in our own time. It examines the wider context of the Bible to resolve problems raised by particular texts, comparing Scripture with Scripture. It also demonstrates the implications for other doctrines if a particular line of interpretation is taken.

Pastoral studies is a potentially vast area and in some training institutions can begin to take precedence over biblical studies or historical and theological pursuits. Important though it is to understand our culture and how to communicate with it, we need to evaluate culture and our methods of communication from a biblical point of view. We need to develop an effective apologetic for biblical faith, learn how to do evangelism, and offer a prophetic-type critique of our society. Every subject such as counselling, leadership, worship, ethics, and pastoral care, ought to be taught from a biblical base, but seriously engaging with contemporary theory and practice. Indeed, pastoral studies cannot legitimately be tacked on to the end of a course of academic study, but ought to be taking place progressively throughout the course. Only in this way can genuine integration of the relevant disciplines be practised.

Potential theological students ought to think carefully about where they will train, asking specific questions of those who teach and those who learn, to discover the reality behind the programme set out in the prospectus. However, no institution is without fault and so students need to accept responsibility for making good what is lacking, and exposing themselves to other helpful influences and experiences. Above all, training needs to be undertaken as an expression of discipleship, with constant prayer to know and serve the Lord Jesus more faithfully. Those who want to follow the model of the apostle Paul will want to grow in godliness, with a special love for God's people, and in knowledge of God's Word and how to apply it.

Where can I train?

Visit the 9:38 website for a recommended list of colleges, and other training schemes: www.ninethirtyeight.org

Where to from here?

Matthew 9 v 38 revisited

Peter Comont

ROGER, CLAIRE, RICHARD AND JONATHAN stumble out of the lecture theatre a little dazed. They have just heard a rousing call to gospel ministry. 'In the light of eternity there is no better way to spend our lives,' said the speaker. The message was compelling, the atmosphere electric, and they were all deeply moved.

Roger is ready to give up his office job tomorrow. He loves leading Bible studies, he has fought more than a few battles for the gospel at university and he is ready for action. He has mentioned his plans to his pastor and was disappointed to have received comments about needing to mature a little more. Perhaps it is one more proof that the greatest opposition to the gospel comes from the church.

Claire, on the other hand is cautious. She has seen God blessing her efforts over the years. More than one friend has been converted. But could she find a full-time job in an evangelical church? Such posts, she knows, are rare for women.

Richard is lost in thought. He knows he would make a competent pastor-teacher but he is also shaping up to be a good doctor. Medicine is his delight. Should he give up the career he loves?

Jonathan brings up the rear. He felt ill at ease among all those gifted and confident go-getters. His heart raced as he heard the speaker, but his spirits slumped as he looked around him. He could never be like them. His mind is not as sharp as theirs, he knows his own private sinfulness. He just feels inadequate. He would love to devote himself to nurturing God's people and proclaiming Christ, but surely he is not good enough.

Where next?

What should these four each do? Although we may be tempted to make a few pertinent observations, it is important for us to recognise that there is no simple answer for any of them. Facets of their characters will have to be probed and tested, realistic questions must be asked, much prayer will be needed. Wise and godly decisions do not come ready packaged off the shelf. However, it is possible for each of them to move forward in the quest to use their lives for God's glory. In fact, a second look at the passage with which we began this book yields some important observations. It is worth revisiting Matthew 9 v 38.

> Jesus went through all the towns and villages, teaching in their synagogues, preaching the good news of the kingdom and healing every disease and sickness. When he saw the crowds, he had compassion on them, because they were harassed and helpless, like sheep without a shepherd. Then he said to his disciples: 'The harvest is plentiful but the workers are few. Ask the Lord of the harvest, therefore, to send out workers into his harvest field.'
>
> **Matthew 9 v 35-38**

The end of chapter 9 is a turning point in Matthew's Gospel. Up to now Jesus has been centre stage, but in Matthew 10, Jesus sends His disciples out for the first time (Matt 10 v 5). This is the beginning of a process which will reach its climax at the end of Matthew's Gospel when the risen Christ finally commissions them to go to all nations (Matt 28 v 18-20). The end of Matthew 9, then, is the moment when Jesus begins to make it plain that He is not going to do everything on His own. His ministry will be completed by his disciples. What can Roger, Claire, Richard and Jonathan learn from this passage?

Word and deed

The first thing we must notice is that Jesus' ministry, and the ministry of His disciples was a ministry of word and deed. Matthew 9 v 35 summarises Jesus' ministry as 'teaching', 'preaching' and 'healing every disease and sickness'. In His life, word ministries of teaching and preaching were integrated with the practical ministry of healing. Together, these pointed to who He was (Acts 10 v 38, 1 John 1 v 3). Moreover, when Jesus commissions His disciples in Matthew 10 they are told to 'drive out evil spirits and heal every disease and sickness' (Matthew 10 v 1) alongside the commission to 'preach' (Matthew 10 v 7).

In the book of Acts and the Epistles, the overtly miraculous dimension of this commission is less prominent and the importance of proclamation is emphasised, but the New Testament writers continue to insist that the deeds of believers are vital in gospel ministry (eg: 1 Peter 2 v 12, 1 Thessalonians 4 v 11-12). Indeed, teaching and preaching are partly to 'prepare God's people for works of service' (Ephesians 4 v 12). The New Testament vision for God's church is that everyone is to work together with their different gifts (1 Corinthians 12 v 12-31), so that together Christ is honoured and proclaimed in word and deed (Colossians 3 v 17, 2 Thessalonians 2 v 17).

This means that Roger, Claire, Richard and Jonathan are not making a choice between a first-class Christian life of Word ministry and a second-class one of something else. God's church desperately needs preachers and teachers, but it also needs godly Christians who will serve in a thousand different jobs and professions. Roger may be unwise to think about Word ministry at present because of his immaturity, but that immaturity will also be a liability in the workplace and could bring disgrace on the name of Christ. It must be addressed. It may be right for Richard to give up medicine, but if he concludes prayerfully that it is not right, and gives his life to faithful service in medicine, he need not think he has chosen second best.

The harvest is close

A second important thing to notice is that the harvest field is closer than we may think. Jesus is prompted to make His observation that 'the harvest is plentiful' as He looks over the crowds in front of Him. He then immediately sends His disciples out to start ministering among the people in the vicinity. It will be some time before they start to make an impact on the wider world, but they are involved in ministry from the start.

This is important for us to absorb, since many people tend to read the call to the harvest field as a call to some distant or future ministry. Countless conferences have used this passage to call missionaries to the other side of the world, or to call people to apply for ordained ministry. The impression is sometimes given that their ministry will begin on the day of ordination, or when they finally set foot on that foreign shore.

But, like charity, gospel ministry begins at home. The harvest field is first our family, our workplace, our friends, our neighbours. Many people try to make decisions about training for full-time word ministry without much personal experience at all. This is very unwise. A theological education is important, but it is not a magic talisman which turns ungifted or unsuitable people into skilled and godly leaders. The primary qualifications for Christian leadership concern character and aptitude (1 Timothy 3 v 1-7, Titus 1 v 6-9), and these should be forged and tested in the furnace of church life, before major decisions are made about ordination or training. My first question to anyone thinking of training for further ministry is: 'What are you doing now?'

In order to gain this vital experience, you need to work closely with local-church leaders. They should be able to offer suitable opportunities, and to discuss and guide you as you are tested and stretched. For many people, such experience is a crucial part of their guidance. If cautious Jonathan should train for church leadership, his confidence in that will grow as he leads a group Bible study and as, perhaps, he preaches occasionally and sees God working in people's lives.

Richard, the doctor, will be able to decide whether he should give up medicine as he commits himself to active service in his church. Roger will know that his pugnacious immaturity is on the wane when he finds himself able to pastor a Bible study group—not just lecture them—and when he finds his office friends asking questions about his faith—not just arguing with him. Claire will learn whether her evangelistic skills will be best used in the workplace or whether she should aim for full-time church work.

Growing our character

But what makes a really effective servant of Christ? Many answers could be given, but Matthew's summary of Jesus' ministry and Jesus' call to His disciples alerts us to some important characteristics that every Christian needs, whatever their ministry.

One vital characteristic is **Christ-like compassion**. 'When he saw the crowds he had compassion on them' (Matthew 9 v 36). No ministry in the name of Christ can be achieved without the love of Christ. A person may be the most able theologian, the most gifted teacher, the most energetic organiser, but without love they will be useless. The apostle Paul tells us that all the gifts in the world, and even life-surrendering commitment, are not worth a thing without love (1 Corinthians 13 v 1-3).

The apostle John, who was present when Jesus looked over these crowds (Matthew 10 v 2), concluded many years later that 'whoever does not love does not know God' (1 John 4 v 8). Matthew here uses a particularly emotional word to describe Jesus' compassion, which is derived from the word for our intestines. Jesus' gut churned with emotion. The apostle Paul later tells us that he experienced the same emotion for the Philippians (Philippians 1 v 8). It is an essential part of the imitation of Christ.

Our time is a time of growing lovelessness, loneliness and pain, in which a thousand 'truths' are peddled in every town. One of the key things which will make the Christian gospel stand out is that it is offered with love. If Christ's love does not compel us (2 Corinthians 5 v 14) then we will be useless as individual disciples, and dangerously destructive as church leaders. Dispassionate ministry is godless ministry.

A second Christ-like characteristic is **spiritual perspective**. When Jesus looked over the crowds He saw what was going on in their hearts. He not only saw them as physically 'harassed and helpless like sheep without a shepherd' (Matthew 9 v 36), He knew that the remedy was the message of the kingdom (Matthew 10 v 7). It is very easy, as we go through life, to lose Christ's perspective. Passionate concern in student days can easily settle into complacent indifference as the years go by.

For the many who do not go into full-time Word ministry, this is distressingly common. The mortgage, the family, and the next promotion become our central concerns. We lose sight of the fact that we are rubbing shoulders every day with lost, spiritually helpless, shepherdless people. Sometimes, even church leaders lose sight of that and opt in their church for maintenance rather than mission. Those who are useful to Christ in the long term are those who keep a true spiritual perspective, whatever job they are in.

A third characteristic which Jesus calls us to is **prayerfulness**. Jesus first calls His disciples to 'ask the Lord of the harvest, therefore, to send out workers' (Matthew 9 v 38). The first part of any work for God is done on our knees. Prayer is an extremely high priority in Scripture, but it is so often overlooked in our active world. The apostles' priority was 'prayer and the ministry of the word' (Acts 6 v 4). Paul calls us to 'pray continually' (1 Thessalonians 5 v 17) about everything (Philippians 4 v 6).

Many people considering full-time Word ministry fondly think that they will have vast stretches of time to pray, and that their present, rather squeezed and desultory prayer life, will be transformed. It is not so. My experience of moving from a demanding professional job to church ministry revealed to me that there are just as many pressures on your time as a pastor, and prayer is just as difficult. If we do not get a grip on our prayer life in the early years of our Christian walk, then it will be enormously difficult to improve it later. Jesus first called His disciples to prayer.

In Matthew 10 Jesus sends His disciples with lengthy instructions about the nature of their ministry, the places they are to go, and the responses they are to expect. Underneath all His instructions, however, is the call to exercise one of the most important Christian characteristics of all. It is courage. They will need courage to trust God for financial support (v 9-10), to live like 'sheep among wolves' (v 16), to face floggings (v 17), slander (v 25) and even death (v 21). They will have to face opposition from rulers (v 18), and religious authorities (v 17) and their own families (v 21, 34-36). It is not surprising that Jesus has to tell them not to worry (v 19), and three times not to be afraid (v 26, 28, 31).

Most of us live in more settled and secure times, but courage is still a vital need. C.S. Lewis writes:

> Courage is not simply one of the virtues, but the form of every virtue at the testing point... a chastity or honesty, or mercy which yields to danger will be chaste or honest of merciful only on conditions. Pilate was merciful till it became risky.

One of the greatest inhibitors to real Christian discipleship is a lack of courage. Financial insecurity can blunt the enthusiasm of many a budding pioneer. Opposition from family, friends or authorities can become insurmountable obstacles. As Lewis says, all other virtues crumble if they are not underpinned with courage. We need to hear Jesus' repeated call not to be afraid and act on it.

Fearing God

One further characteristic which makes a disciple of Christ unassailably useful is a commitment to live life before an audience of One. Jesus' encouragements to His disciples do not concern the great ministries they will have, nor does He promise them immunity from trials, disappointments, frustration and danger. His encouragements are all about God's attitude to them.

He is the one to be feared because He can destroy both body and soul in hell (Matt 10 v 28), and yet, He is the one who treasures them more than many sparrows (v 31). He is the one who gives true life (v 39) and rewards even our smallest deeds (v 42). In the end God's opinion of us is all that matters. This is a truly liberating truth. Fear puts a cage around us, but once we have learned to fear only God, we are set free. A thousand things in this world may threaten us but we need not fear even death itself if we are loved by the living God. Other people may estimate our life as worthless, but that matters nothing if God is looking on and noting our every action with pleasure.

There is an irresistible joy, peace and fruitfulness in a Christian who has learned to live in this way. A Christian who has learned to feel Christ's compassion and to see with Christ's perspective, who has learned to pray faithfully, and live courageously only to please God, will not go far wrong.

Our subject was: 'Where to from here?' Perhaps the first answer is to our knees, then to Christ, and then to ministry in our current situation, in word and deed, under the guidance of our local church leaders. If we live our lives for Christ today He will make our future paths straight (Proverbs 3 v 5-6).

SECTION 4:
Appendices

This article by Chris Green, Vice Principal of Oak Hill Theological College, is aimed at local church ministers: to encourage them to take seriously their responsibility to pray for, identify, develop and support people for Christian ministry.

The other Lord's Prayer

Christopher Green

> Jesus went through all the towns and villages, teaching in their synagogues, preaching the good news of the kingdom and healing every disease and sickness. When he saw the crowds, he had compassion on them, because they were harassed and helpless, like sheep without a shepherd. Then he said to his disciples: 'The harvest is plentiful but the workers are few. Ask the Lord of the harvest, therefore, to send out workers into his harvest field.'
>
> **Matthew 9 v 35-38**

A great time to be a worker

Our world, says Jesus, is lost and leaderless. Echoing the criticisms of the prophets, He denounced the religious and political leadership of Israel for failing to care for their sheep. Those who should be overseen and protected were wandering. And this was no happy freedom; in His words *the lost people were 'harassed and helpless'*.

So the great Shepherd-King came (Ezekiel 34 v 11, Zechariah 11 v 16). Jesus Himself shouldered the duties of the missing shepherds, and initiated a time when salvation could be offered to all the nations. And in the scene which follows this section, He appointed the Twelve as the basis for a renewed people of God with renewed shepherds under His care.

The apostles' foundational ministry would need to spread further than Israel for the whole world to come under Jesus' universal kingship, and so He tells them His second view of our world: *it's full of people ready for 'harvest'*.

That double view, a double agricultural image of people utterly lost like unpastored sheep, but ripe and ready for collection like heavy heads of corn, is one that has not changed. Today is still a day of unparalleled need and unparalleled opportunity.

And so the requirement Jesus identified runs on. He intends to replace those absent shepherds with new ones who will work with Him. Even the Twelve will not be adequate for this task because 'the workers are few'. Jesus has outlined the greatest need and greatest opportunity in world history, and He needs many more people to join the work of pastoring the sheep and gathering the harvest. It's a great day to be a worker because it's the gospel day.

Are you praying for workers?

Since neither the need nor the mandate has changed, Jesus' solution must still stand too: 'Ask the Lord of the harvest, therefore, to send out workers into his harvest field' (Matthew 9 v 38). *We are to pray for the provision of workers.*

This is Jesus' *other* Lord's Prayer, and it's one we hardly use in our churches. As Christians, we often ask one another: 'What should we pray for?'—and yet, here is a direct command and framework from Jesus Himself. Is this a day of lost people, false shepherds, but still the day of the gospel? Then we should obediently start praying for workers.

As you pray for the congregation you are part of, is this one of your constant prayers?

• *Do you see the world around you as lost and leaderless?*

- *Do you see their need for workers?*

- *Do you ask the Lord of the harvest to send out workers?*

Are you training workers?

> But you know that Timothy has proved himself, because as a son
> with his father he has served with me in the work of the gospel.
>
> **Philippians 2 v 22**

The concept of the *work* and *workers* carried over from Jesus to the early church, and are terms found frequently in the New Testament. Paul's strategy in recruiting, training and deploying church workers can be clearly traced in Acts, most obviously in Timothy. Here was an enormously gifted young man, whom Paul took under his wing at the recommendation of the church (Acts 16 v 1-3), and who learnt both theology and good pastoral practice (2 Timothy 3 v 10-17) over a number of years. He learnt by being close to good teaching and by being sent out on his own, whether to friendly or hostile settings (Philippians 2 v 19-23, 1 Corinthians 16 v 10-11).

This was a pattern which Timothy was to put into practice (2 Timothy 1 v 13), and which it is clear Paul expected Timothy to expect of others (2 Timothy 2 v 2). So here is a second set of challenges for today:

- *Are you, like the church at Lystra, actively nurturing and seeking out the next generation of workers from among your members?*

- *Are you spending time with them to make sure that they have a good theological grasp and a range of ministry experiences?*

- *Having prayed that God will raise up workers, are you expecting Him to answer that prayer from among your current membership, and are you ready to have an apprentice when He does?*

Are you supporting future workers?

> The elders who direct the affairs of the church well are worthy of double honour, especially those whose work is preaching and teaching. For the Scripture says, 'Do not muzzle the ox while it is treading out the grain,' and 'The worker deserves his wages'.
> **1 Timothy 5 v 17-18**

These workers will spend the majority of their time in preaching and teaching, and so it's important that they have the skills and reliability to do that properly (2 Timothy 2 v 2). Workers who have reliability without ability will bore people, but workers who have ability without reliability will become plausible false teachers. To ensure that the *workers* are able to do the job faithfully, they need appropriate training. And to acquire that they need time and money.

Someone who cuts off a promising career to work with a church part-time and explore what full-time church work might mean needs a salary. Someone who decides to spend time at a theological college needs money. Independent students and Church of England ordinands who want to stay more than the bare minimum of time need extra funding.

Being obedient to what the Bible says about producing workers will mean more than praying for and identifying workers; it will mean your church agreeing to fund them realistically.

Are you clear on what workers need to know?

> Do your best to present yourself to God as one approved, a workman who does not need to be ashamed and who correctly handles the word of truth. **2 Timothy 2 v 15**

The workers we all need are to do one task above all: to teach the Bible well. That means having a careful look at the kind of training available and choosing the best on this criterion: *is this a programme which will equip someone for a life-long ministry of faithful*

Bible teaching? Quite clearly, that was what Paul gave Timothy, and what he expected Timothy to live up to and to build into others. It is the key question to ask.

It is vital that potential workers learn early on that this will be their primary and life-long task, and to evaluate every aspect of their ministry training in the light of it. Such training will include how the Bible is communicated publicly and privately, to a large crowd or a grieving daughter, to a new Christian or on a denominational committee. But the heart of the training must be a correct and deep understanding of the Bible.

Deep understanding of the Bible leads to better understanding of other subjects, and good workers need a wide grasp of theology too: *Biblical theology* will help them put the entire Bible together in a coherent pattern; *Systematic theology* helps them sort the Biblical material into relevant areas and themes; *Historical theology* helps them understand how previous generations of Christians tackled their own burning issues, just as *ethics* tackles our own.

Good training involves discerning how our world understands itself and how to communicate to it, as well as how to plant, lead and pastor mission-oriented churches that will make the next generation of disciples. The Bible stands at the centre of all these disciplines, controlling and informing them, but they each need studying in their own right, and that takes time. The Church of England, for example, requires a minimum of two years, and we at Oak Hill prefer to say a minimum of three. It really does take that long to gain the basic skills. To fall short at this point is to undercut all the good work that has gone on in the home church.

Those who have had poor theological training themselves must surely be concerned that the next generation receives the best training possible. Although we all recognise the importance of practical training for full-time ministry, evangelicals ought to give the highest priority to Biblical and theological development.

A strategy for obedience

What, then, is your church going to do to produce the workers our churches need for the future? What we have seen suggests a five-fold plan, which every congregation should have as part of its obedient strategy for making disciples.

Praying

- *Ask God regularly to raise up workers.*

Identifying

- *Expect Him to answer your prayers from among your congregation.*

Recruiting

- *Take such people under your wing to give them theological and ministerial depth. For information and support, contact an organisation like 9:38 (see contact details in Appendix II)*

Resourcing

- *Provide the money for them to have the fully-rounded training they need.*

Training

- *Ensure that the training they have will equip them to handle God's Word properly and in depth, otherwise you are wasting your prayers, their time, and your church's money.*

APPENDIX II
9:38

9:38 is a national evangelical interdenominational charity,
which has been established to help people consider whether
paid gospel ministry might be for them.

What's our vision?
That many gifted and godly men and women would be identified,
recruited, trained and sent out to take the gospel of Jesus Christ to
those living in this country and overseas.

How do we do it?

Apprenticeship Schemes
Apprenticeship schemes are one- or two-year placements with
Bible-teaching churches, to provide good practical experience of
gospel ministry. The focus is on helping individuals understand
and train for the sort of gospel work that is suitable for them.

Apprenticeships aim to act both as a testing of the water of
whether full-time gospel ministry is right for the apprentice, and
as a stepping-stone into full-time gospel ministry if it is right for
them. These placements will provide great experience of gospel
ministry, in a context of training and mentoring, that will help in
discerning whether gospel ministry is for the apprentice or not.
UK based apprenticeships are run by local churches and the aim is
that the church has the attitude of 'train, train, train' and the
apprentice the attitude of 'serve, serve, serve'.

Each apprenticeship will have the following three main components in different proportions, depending on the individual situation of the particular church:

- Practical service
- Bible and ministry training
- Word ministry

There are currently over 200 apprenticeships in the UK with around 100 churches. The majority of apprentices are men and women who have just graduated (but more and more are older), and there are now some opportunities that are part-time.

Conferences

All our conferences include Bible teaching, seminars on specific ministries and a chance to chat one-to-one with local church leaders and other gospel ministers.

Talks outline what the Bible says about ministry and who should be engaged in it. Seminars in the past have included: international mission; marriage, singleness and ministry; youth and children's work; Free Church ministry; Anglican ministry; women's ministry and ministry in Urban Priority Areas.

There are lots of opportunities to get to know like-minded people who are thinking through similar issues and to chat with experienced church leaders and workers who are able to share advice and wisdom. Anyone going on a conference must have the support of their church pastor.

Annual Conferences

To help people who are in the workplace to consider paid full-time or part-time gospel ministry now or in the future.

Student Conference

To help students think through the principles of paid gospel ministry and whether it might be right for them.

Apprentice Conference

This conference is especially for apprentices: to encourage and equip them for their gospel ministry now and in the future; and to build a peer group of like-minded gospel workers

Please pray that the Lord of the harvest would send out workers into the harvest field.

Keeping in touch

9:38 produce a quarterly newsletter keeping you up to date with news and upcoming events, articles on gospel work being done all over the country, and insights into the life of an apprentice.

If you would like to receive the newsletter free of charge, sign up on the website.

Check out the website for information, articles, apprenticeships, jobs and details on the conferences.

---

www.ninethirtyeight.org

For more information on 9:38 contact the administrator at:

admin@ninethirtyeight.org

01865 204879

2 Roger Bacon Lane

Oxford OX1 1QE

Routes to full-time ministry

There is a huge variety of practical ways in which individual churches and denominations organise their recruitment systems—many of them marked by their length or obscurity. The basic process for the Church of England is outlined below:

1. Church minister supports your application and contacts the Diocesan Director of Ordinands (DDO)

⬇

2. A series of interviews with the DDO. This can take a year or more.

⬇

3. If DDO approves of your application, interview with the Bishop

⬇

4. If approved, you are sent to a Bishop's Advisory Panel (BAP) conference. *They make the decision to recommend or not*

⬇

5. If recommended, the Church of England will pay for training.

⬇

6. On ordination, there is a training post (curacy) for 3 or 4 years.

There are other, similar schemes operated by the larger denominations, and by mission agencies, which have rigorous procedures for interviewing and vetting applicants. In denominations with a more congregational or presbyterian structure, for example, the recommendation for training for ministry will depend more heavily on the support of the whole church, or of the churches in an area.

The situation in independent evangelical churches is a little more arbitrary, but the structure of the route is essentially the same. The minister, or elders, will interview the candidate, and either make the recommendation themselves, or else present the candidate to the whole church for them to vote upon.

Support for, and the kind of, ministry training encouraged, also varies immensely. Some churches will enrol the candidate as a full-time assistant pastor from the start, and mix and match some training over the next few years before encouraging them to apply for a pastorate elsewhere. Other churches will encourage a formal training period at a preferred college before beginning in any formal role.

In all cases, however, the process really starts with informal ministry experience leading to discussions with, and a recommendation by, the leadership of the local church.

CONTRIBUTORS

Vaughan Roberts is the Rector of St Ebbe's Church, Oxford.

Tim Thornborough is Publisher at The Good Book Company.

David Jackman is the President of the Proclamation Trust.

Richard Coekin is the senior minister of the Co-Mission initiative—a group of churches in SW London.

Andy Gemmill is the pastor of Beeston Free Church, Nottingham.

Roger Carswell is an itinerant evangelist based in Leeds.

Tim Chester is an editor and writer, and is part of the Crowded House church planting initiative.

Andy Lines worked as a missionary in Paraguay, and is now General Secretary of Crosslinks.

Andrew Raynes is the minister of Christ Church, Blackburn.

Carrie Sandom is the women's worker at The Bible Talks, a church in central London.

Roger Fawcett is the youth and children's worker at St John's Church, Hertford.

Ken Molder is Vicar of St Oswald's Church, Newcastle-upon-Tyne.

Nathan Buttery is Associate and Student Minister at St. John's Newland, Hull.

Christopher Ash is Director of the Cornhill Training Course.

Ian Garrett runs the apprenticeship scheme at Jesmond Parish Church, Newcastle-upon-Tyne.

David Peterson is the Principal of Oak Hill Theological College.

Peter Comont ministers at Magdalen Road Church, Oxford.

Christopher Green is Vice-Principal of Oak Hill Theological College.